Participant's Guide

REJOICE in RECOVERY

A 12-Step
Faith-Based Program

Marjorie J. Wynn, Ph.D.

Rejoice in Recovery
A 12-Step Faith-Based Program *(RNR)*
Participant's Guide
Copyright 2014 Marjorie J. Wynn
mjwynn29@gmail.com

ISBN-13
978-1497563889
ISBN-10
1497563887

Cover Image: 123rf.com/sokolovanton'
Cover Design: Elizabeth Little, Hyliian Graphics

Scripture quotations are taken from the Holy Bible, New Living Translation, copyright ©1996, 2004, 2007, 2013 by Tyndale House Foundation. Used by permission of Tyndale House Publishers, Inc., Carol Stream, Illinois 60188. All rights reserved.

The Life Recovery Bible (LRB), New Living Translation, second edition, published by Tyndale House Publishers was used when developing this program. Page numbers for scripture and footnote references are for the *LRB.*

Other Bible translations may also be used with the *RNR* program in which case referenced page numbers will not apply.

The Twelve Steps are adapted from The Twelve Steps of Alcoholics Anonymous and are used here with permission of Alcoholics Anonymous World Services, Inc. (AAWS). Permission to adapt The Twelve Steps does not mean that AAWS has reviewed or approved the contents of this publication, or that AAWS necessarily agrees with the views expressed herein. AA is a program of recovery from alcoholism *only*-use of the Twelve Steps in connection with programs and activities which are patterned after AA, but which address other problems, or in any other non-AA context, does not imply otherwise.

Ellen Sallas *The Author's Mentor (www.ellencmaze.com)* provided invaluable advice, services, and suggestions for the publication of *RNR.* I am indebted to Ellen for her patience, persistence, and thought-provoking cover design.

Dedication

RNR is dedicated to:

Gwen Henderson: a leading expert in the field of addiction, our self-selected daughter, mentor, and friend, who taught me almost everything I know about the trials, tribulations, and triumphs of recovery and *forced* me to memorize *The Big Book of Alcoholics Anonymous*.

Participants: voluntary class members, instrumental in the development of *RNR* - who spent innumerable hours reading their Bibles, responding to homework questions, discussing what they learned, and making suggestions for curriculum changes - in the

*Cumberland County Jail - Crossville, Tennessee
*First Baptist Church - Prescott, Arizona

These participants faced *Goliath-challenges* and discovered:
*Anyone who belongs to Christ has become a new person.
The old life is gone. A **new life** has begun!* (2 Corinthians 5: 17)

RNR Leadership Teaching Teams: men and women whose hard work and dedication will be forever remembered and cherished by class participants. These special people answered the Lord's call:
*The harvest is great, but the workers are few.
So pray to the Lord who is in charge of the harvest:
Ask Him to send more workers into His fields."* (Luke 10:2)

Vonette Murphy: a pastor's wife with a shepherd's heart - who called, captured the *RNR* vision, and came to my house with men and women ready, willing, and able to implement *RNR* in the
*White County Jail - Sparta, Tennessee
*Doyle United Methodist Church - Doyle, Tennessee

Chuck Wynn: my phenomenal husband, special friend, and non-stop encourager who has supported me at all times during the *ups-and-downs* of this challenging, at times frustrating, exasperating, ministry. Chuck has spent innumerable hours brainstorming teaching ideas, proofreading yet another manuscript, and listening patiently as I *fuss-and-almost-cuss* about yet another relapse.

God: my God who called me and I answered…reluctantly - like Moses at the burning bush, "You want me do what? BUT God…" And after enumerating the reasons why I was NOT the person *fit-for-the-task*, I said, "Yes, Lord!" and have been blessed beyond measure.

An Introduction to Rejoice in Recovery

Tell me, I forget
Show me, I remember.
Involve me, I understand.
(ancient Chinese proverb)

Rejoice in Recovery: A 12-Step Faith-Based Program (RNR) is specifically designed for men and women caught in the grip of drug and alcohol addiction. Over the past ten years, this program has been implemented in church and jail-based recovery classes.

Stories are one of the most effective strategies for teaching and one of the most powerful ways to learn. When we hear, "Once upon a time…," we lean forward and listen with rapt attention and great anticipation, because we know a story is sure to follow. Jesus, the greatest teacher the world has ever known, consistently used stories as a method of instruction so that people would understand and remember the spiritual truths He was teaching. Like Jesus we too can use stories, His stories, to teach and learn life-lessons.

Traditional 12-step programs have a positive tract record in guiding the recovery experience for thousands of people. These programs follow the principles and spiritual values found in the Bible, specifically: *The Sermon on the Mount; The Book of James; and 1 Corinthians 13 (Dick B. 2005)*. Studying the steps, while examining their biblical principles, will guide in discovering why they have been effective and how they can be instructional on our recovery journey.

Alcoholics Anonymous (AA) and *Narcotics Anonymous (NA)* include an abundance of personal recovery stories. Why? True-life experiences teach us, in a way no lecture or essay can, how to make changes in our lives that will positively impact our journey on the road to recovery.

RNR incorporates the power of biblical stories with the principles and spiritual values of 12-step programs. Some unique components of RNR are:

- ***Step-Story Integration:** Interweaves a different Bible story with each of the 12 steps. Within each of the selected stories, a central figure makes some tragic mistakes. Then, through an attention intervention, God provides an invitation for transformation.

   *Participant's Guide: Includes a chapter for each step with thought-provoking information and a wide-variety of user-friendly question-response formats. Many of the questions challenge us to come face-to-face with ourselves while taking a tough, honest look at what we've done in the past, where we are now, and how we are going to make changes for our futures. Information from *AA* and *NA* is included. There is a weekly check sheet for our daily devotions, Bible reading, homework/journaling, and prayer requests. In addition, *something-to-think-about* selections include samples of participants' work.

Rejoice in Recovery Contents Participant's Guide

Note: STTA: Something-to-Think-About

Something-to-Think-About (STTA) Index

STTA: Quality Quotes

*L. B., Inmate, Tennessee Prison for Women (TPFW), Nashville, Tennessee
Before I got put in jail, I'm not even sure that I believed in our God. After getting locked up, I started going to Margie's church services and was still very pessimistic. As time passed, and I continued to read my Bible, I became much more interested. Then Margie started her life changing 12-Step Program. I say this, because it's the reason I'm saved. Later as a child of God, I got baptized. Margie always expected more out of me than I thought I could give such as memorizing Bible verses and the 12 steps. To this day I still remember those verses and steps word-for-word. Following the 12 steps the way I was taught in Margie's class works. Of course, I'd get mad sometimes and want to give up, but Margie was always there to give encouragement and advice. I can truly say I never thought I would be doing a 12-step program, but I took Margie's classes 3 times. I would probably have continued taking them, but I got transferred to TPFW. The class teaches self-discipline, confidence in self and in others, faith, how to heal buried pain, and much more. RNR is a 12-step faith-based program that has and will continue to change lives.

*J. B., Inmate, Cumberland County Jail, Crossville, Tennessee
The class homework has made me able to take a long hard look at my life and examine my heart deep within, even those deep hidden places, and turn it all over to God. I am getting into God's word and evaluating my own self. I am so much closer to the Lord. I understand the Bible much more because of the homework. My prayer life has grown and is out of this world! *Note: I had worked with J. B. several times in the past. This time she came in tough and not really interested in what was going on in the class. Since the class is voluntary, I was surprised she came at all. During the second class, I noticed that J. B. didn't take her eyes off me. Her face/demeanor had softened. I stopped teaching, looked at her, and said, "J. B., you're different. You've changed." The tears started and almost didn't stop. When I asked her later what had happened to change her, she said, "The homework sucked me in."*

*M. K., Recovery House
Ms. Margie's class led me to God. You see, I was an atheist, and then I took Ms. Margie's *(jail)* class. She showed me through her teaching and her class that I can overcome my addictions. She taught me that I can be a joyful, happy, sober person. Working the steps in her class has benefited my life so much. So what I got out of Ms. Margie's class was a new life and a new way of thinking about and coping with my addictions. I have been sober for 10 months *(much longer now)*. So what I got was a sober life, and God in my life.

E. R., Inmate, Silverdale Correctional Facility, Chattanooga, Tennessee
It's hard to believe that it's been close to a year since we first met. Your 12-step RNR program helped plant a seed in my heart. I think I'm growing up. I have seen the errors of my ways and am ashamed. But I'm working on me now, finding out who I am without drugs, sex, and rock & roll…I appreciate all that you do (first & foremost-you making me feel like a human being; letting me know that, *"All have sinned and fallen short of the glory of God."* Thanks.

Rejoice in Recovery 12-Step Faith-Based Study
Participant's Lesson
Step # 1   **Date** _____
"For I know the plans I have for you," says the Lord.
"They are plans for good and not for disaster, to give you a future and a hope."
Jeremiah 29:11

*Step #1 Smart Start: *Devotionals start on page 25 LR Bible*
*Step #1:   "I can't!"
        We _____ that we were _____ over our _____-
        that our lives had become _____.
*Step #1 Paraphrase: *Alcohol/drugs will kill me*
*Step #1 Key Terms: *Admit, denial, honesty, justification, lying, manipulation,*
                powerless, rationalization, unmanageable

*Step #1 Chant:
        *Lie to **me**. Lie to **you**.*   *Lie to **God**, and **others** too.*
        ***Honesty**! Honesty!*   *Is what God, expects from me.*
        *I will **lose** (3X)*   *If I choose to use.*
        *I will **win** (3X)*   *If I let God in. (Step #3)*

*Step #1 Introduction: What should you do when you get to the *end-of-your-rope*?

1.   When I tell myself the **truth**, I **admit** my responsibility for my decisions and
      actions. What is the truth I should I tell myself about my addictive lifestyle?

2.   Unfortunately I am often **dishonest** with myself and with others. Why do I **lie**?

3.   **Subtle ways** you can lie: *Examples from your life:*
      *Mislead (changing details)   *
      *Omission (leaving something out)   *
      *Failure to correct misunderstanding   *

4.   **Who** do I lie to?   **What** have I lied about?
      *   *
      *   *
      *   *
      *   *

5.   Share times when you lied, when you felt it was **inconsequential**, *wouldn't make
      any difference,* whether or not you told the truth.
      *
      *
      *

6.   Who did I **hurt** when I lied?
      *   *
      *   *

7.   When is it **O.K.** to lie?

8.   How can lying become a bad habit, a ***way-of-life***?

9. What does the **Bible** say about lying?
Proverbs 12: 22 *(p. 799)*
*The Lord detests **lying** lips,*
*But He delights in those who tell the **truth**.*

Proverbs 28 1:b <u>The Message Bible</u>
***Honest** people are*
relaxed and confident.

Colossians 3: 9-10 *(p. 1534)*
***Don't lie** to each other,*
For you have stripped off your old
sinful nature and all its wicked deeds.

Truth-Telling Tactics
When tempted to lie, here are 3 things I will do to help me tell the truth:

* _____
_____

* _____
_____

* _____
_____

10. **Denial** is *lying to myself and telling myself I don't have a problem.* For example, "I don't have a drug problem, and even if I did, it's not my fault. I can quit anytime I want to." What are you in denial about regarding your addictions?
    *

    *

11. **Rationalization** is *a way of lying to myself or others in which I give what appear to be reasonable, but less-than-honest explanations for why I do what I do.* For example, "I've really got a bad headache, so I'll just take a couple of pills to help me get through the day." How do you rationalize your addictions?
    *

    *

12. **Justification** is *a way of lying to myself or others in which I make what I'm doing O.K. and attempt to appear guilt-free.* For example, "My drug use is not hurting me or anyone else." How do you attempt to justify your addictions?
    *

    *

13. **Manipulation** is used *to convince others to do what I want them to do.* For example, "You know I love you and only you. If you really love me, you'll get those pills for me. Don't worry. If you're caught, I'll take the charge." Share personal examples of when you manipulated others to get what you wanted.
    *

    *

14. When I have **power**, *I'm the one in control.* I am doing *what* I want to, *when* I want to, and *how* I want to. What are some people, places, or things over which you have power?
    *
    *

15.   When I am **powerless**, *I'm not the one in control*. I can't do *what* I want to, *when* I want to, and *how* I want to. What are some people, places, or things over which I am powerless?
        *
        *
        *

16.   What is the evidence that I **want** to have power over my addiction, but I have been unsuccessful?

17.   What is the evidence that my life is **unmanageable**, that my life has *spun-out-of- control*?

.

*Step # 1 Memory Verse: *Jonah 2: 2a (p. 1138)*
                *I cried out to the **Lord** in my great **trouble**, and He **answered** me.*
1.   What has to happen in my life to make me willing to cry out to God and do what He tells me to do? _____
_____

2.   I have practiced writing this verse on the margins of this page and other pages in the homework _____ times and know this verse from memory. _____
                                                                        Signature

*Step #1 Extra Credit Verse: *Jeremiah 29: 11 (p. 970)*
                *For I know the **plans** I have for you says the **Lord**.*
                *They are plans for **good** and not for **disaster**,*
                *to give you a **future** and a **hope**.*

1.   My Plans: Past, Present, and Future
*What kind of plans/dreams did I have in the past before my addictions took over my life? _____
_____

*What has interfered with these plans/dreams? _____
_____

*What plans/dreams does God have for my future? _____
_____

*What plans/dreams do I have for my future? _____
_____

2.   I have practiced writing this verse on the margins of this page and other pages in the homework _____ times and know this verse from memory. _____
                                                                        Signature

*Step #1 Bible Story: Jonah the *Pity-Pot* Prophet
Read Jonah: Chapters 1-4 *(pp. 1135-1140)*
Jonah was a man who said, "No!" to God. He got in big trouble and ended up in his own personal jail/prison, the belly of a whale.* He found out pretty quickly that he was **powerless** over his predicament, and that his life was **unmanageable**. See what you can learn from Jonah and how you can apply what you learn to your own life. (**great fish*)

*Chapter 1: Jonah Rebels

1.   When God said, "Go *this-a-way*." What did Jonah do?

2.   When God said, "Do this…my way!" what was Jonah's attitude?

3.   Examples of when you said, "No!" to God and went in the opposite direction:
When: *What happened:*
*   *

*   *

4.   Who did Jonah's rebellion/disobedience affect?

5.   Who does your rebellion affect, and how do you feel about this?
Who: *Your feelings:*
*   *

*   *

*   *

6.   What kind of an **attention intervention**, *Stop! Look! Listen! Choose-to-Change Experience*, did God use to get Jonah's attention?

7.   How does God get your attention?   Impact on you?
*   *
*   *
*   *

***Jonah's motto: I can't! I won't!! You can't make me!!!*
*Chapter 2: Jonah Requests

1.   God gave Jonah a time-out to contemplate the consequences of his bad choices. What did Jonah do while he was in the belly of the great fish and dealing with an insurmountable problem?

2.   Share a time when God gave you a time-out to contemplate the consequences of your bad choices, and share what you did to overcome your insurmountable problems.

3.   God did a great miracle in Jonah's life when he was *going down for the last time.* Jonah said, "But you, O Lord my God, snatched me from the jaws of death!" *(vs. 6b)* **Share** a personal experience when you were *going down for the last time,* and **God** miraculously **snatched you** from the jaws of death.

4.   The sailors worshipped false gods *(vs. 8)*. False gods or **idols** are *anything or anyone we put before God and give affection and/or obedience to*. Who/what are some false gods in your life:

*   *

*   *

*   *

5.   Jonah praised the Lord for his salvation *(vs. 9)*.
*What is salvation? _____
*What would you like to know about salvation? _____
_____

6.   What are some things you praise/thank the Lord for?
*   *

*   *

*   *

7.   How did Jonah get out of the belly of the fish?

*Chapter 3: Jonah Reconsiders
1.   When God gave Jonah a second-chance, what did Jonah do?

2.   **Repent** involves choosing-to-change your: (1) head, (2) heart, and (3) direction. How will your life **change** if you **repent** and start going in the opposite direction?

3.   What are some examples from your life when God gave you a second chance?
*

*

*

4.   After hearing Jonah's message, what was the response of the people in Nineveh?

*Chapter 4: Jonah Regrets
1.   God decided not to destroy Nineveh. What was Jonah's response to God's change of plans? _____

2.   Why do you think Jonah responded this way?

3. Share a situation in which God appeared to be blessing someone you knew did **not** deserve to be blessed.

4. Jonah had a *sit-and-sulk-pity-party*. For this party God created a shelter, a leafy plant, for Jonah to sit under, but then God arranged for a worm to eat through the stem of the plant destroying Jonah's shade. What was Jonah learning the hard way?

5. Our addiction is a *shelter from the pain in our lives.* When our shelter, *addiction,* is removed, we get angry, and our hidden character defects are revealed *(see Jonah devotional on page 1139).* What are the **real problems** your addictions are hiding, and how can you **deal** with these problems more effectively rather than going back to your addictions?

Real problems addiction/s hiding: *How to deal with more effectively:*
*   *

*   *

*   *

*Application
1. What happened when Jonah tried to do things his own way?
   (Hint: footnote 2: 1-10; choice n' consequences)

2. When did Jonah get to the point that he realized he was <u>powerless</u> and his life had become <u>unmanageable</u>? *(Step #1)*

3. What <u>changes</u> did Jonah make in his life?

4. How are you like the <u>old</u> Jonah?

5. How are you like the <u>new</u> Jonah?

6. How is being in prison/jail, like being in the belly of a whale *(great fish)*?

7. How do you know when you get to the point that you accept that you are <u>powerless</u> and your life has become <u>unmanageable</u>? *(Step #1)*

*Jonah's New Motto: *I can! I will!! I'll obey You!!!*

*Step #1: Did You Get It?

Please circle True or False, and **explain why** you made each choice:

Three pertinent ideas AA Big Book *(based on page 60)*

1. I am an/a <u>alcoholic</u> *(drug addict)* and cannot manage my own life.   True   False

2. Through my own will I can relieve my <u>alcoholism</u> *(drug addiction)*.   True   False

3. God can and will relieve my <u>alcoholism</u> *(drug addiction)* if I seek Him.   True   False

NA Information *(based on pp. 18-22)*

1. I am sure I want to stop <u>using</u>.   True   False

2. I understand that I have no real control over <u>drugs</u>.   True   False

3. I recognize that in the long run, I don't use <u>drugs</u>,
   they use me.   True   False

4. Jails/prisons and institutions have taken over the
   management of my life at different times.   True   False

5. I fully accept the fact that my every attempt to stop
   <u>using</u> or to control my <u>using</u> failed.   True   False

6. I know that my <u>addiction</u> changed me into someone
   I didn't want to be: dishonest, deceitful, a self-willed
   person at odds with myself and my fellow man.   True   False

7. I believe I am a failure.   True   False

8. I am able to live with or without <u>drugs</u>.   True   False

9. I can control my addiction, therefore I can control my life.   True False

10. I believe that it's not where I have been that counts,
    but where I am going.   True   False

12/12 Information *(based on pp. 21-24)*

1. I don't have to hit bottom before I can start going up.   True   False

2. I don't have to be <u>powerless;</u> I can fix my own life.   True   False

3. I must step out of denial and accept the fact that my life
   is <u>unmanageable,</u> thus out-of- control.   True   False

4. Before I can start on the road to recovery,
   I must admit complete defeat.   True   False

*Step #1 Reflections:

1.   Am I at the point that I am willing to **admit** that I, by myself, am **powerless** over my addiction? Am I willing to confront my addiction head-on? Am I willing to go to any length to battle my addiction? If so, what are my **honest** answers to the following questions? *(based on NA pp. 18-19)*

*Do I want to stop using?   _____

*Do I understand that I have no real control over drugs?   _____

*Do I recognize that in the long run, I didn't use drugs, they used me.   _____

*Did jails/prisons or institutions take over management of my life at different times?____

*Do I accept the fact that my every attempt to stop using or control my use failed? _____

*Do I know that my addiction changed me into someone I didn't want to be: dishonest, deceitful, self-willed, a person at odds with myself and others?   _____

*How have I hit bottom *physically*? _____

*How have I hit bottom *mentally*? _____

*How have I hit bottom *spiritually*? _____

*How committed am I to changing my life? _____

2.   Who did you share Step #1 and Jonah's story with _____
Reactions? _____

3.   Please share 3 **new goals** you have for your life when you are released from jai/prison and steps you are going to take to reach these goals:

Goals:	*Steps to reach goals:*
*	*
*	*
*	*

Please complete the following check sheet during the week:

Name _____   _____ Class

Dates: _____   _____ Brought Bible/Pencil

Class/Church Attendance   _____ Brought Extra Credit

Date: Class/Church Name: _____ Brought Journal

Date:	Class/Church Name:
_____	_____
_____	_____
_____	_____
_____	_____
_____	_____

Memory Practice Step #1

_____ Step #1

_____ Memory Verse

_____ Extra Cr. Memory Verse

Devotions begin on p. 25	Bible Reading	Homework for Step #1
_____ Devotional #1	_____ Day #1	_____ Day #1
_____ Devotional #2	_____ Day #2	_____ Day #2
_____ Devotional #3	_____ Day #3	_____ Day #3
_____ Devotional #4	_____ Day #4	_____ Day #4
_____ Devotional #5	_____ Day #5	_____ Day #5
_____ Devotional #6	_____ Day #6	_____ Day #6
_____ Devotional #7	_____ Day #7	_____ Day #7

Please write your prayer requests below:

STTA: **Good-bye Drugs: Poetry Letters**

> 2012 Set-Free Lane
> Golden Gate, TN 38500
> Drug Addiction

#1 Loser-of-My-Life Dr.
Doomstown, TN 38506

Good-Bye Drugs,
I hate you with a passion you'll never know,
But I keep coming back to you, as if it isn't so.
> My addiction to your power seems impossible to tame.
> Regardless of what I believe, it always turns out the same.
On my way to be with you, I say it's my last time.
Unable to say, "No," until I've spent my last dime.
> I'll do anything to be with you, no matter the cost.
> There is no way I can ever get back all I've lost.
I continue thinking about you, no matter what I do.
Pondering where I would be in life if it weren't for you.
> I met you many years ago. I'll never forget the day.
> I'd do anything to go back again, say, "No," and walk away.
Unfortunately things aren't that easy, but there's something you should know.
It's a waste of time to tempt me now,
Because God is in charge, and with Him my life will finally grow.
> *Good-bye forever,*   C. W.

>   To: Dope   No Hope Dr.   Loserville, TN
Dear Dope,
I look back at all the time we spent together.
> All the parties we crashed.
> All the pipes we smashed.
We had days of endless fun…
That always kept me on the run.
> Family and responsibilities did not seem to matter none-
> Especially since you were riding shotgun.
Remember the night we went to jail?
I'm still here-guess you made bail.
> We had a good time; you had your fun.
> All the crying is done.
It's a sad lonely sound when the gavel comes down.
I've got 6 years to give, so I won't be around,
But it's OK cause a better friend I have found.
> Jesus is the reason I can let you go,
> And I can say farewell to you dear dope.
> Cause with you I realized there is no hope.
This is goodbye. I don't need to get high. Just to get by.
I have so many other things to occupy my time.
> *Sincerely, no longer your friend.*   T. P.

Rejoice in Recovery 12-Step Faith-Based Study
Participant's Lesson
Step #2   **Date** _____
"For I know the plans I have for you," says the Lord.
"They are plans for good and not for disaster, to give you a future and a hope."
Jeremiah 29:11

*Step #2 Smart Start: *Devotionals start on page 651 LR Bible*
*Step #2   God can!   *Draw:*
We came to _____   *Believe in heart*
that a _____ greater than _____   *Draw source of help/hope*
could restore us to _____.   *Sane brain*

*Step #2 Paraphrase: *There's a Power that wants me to live.*
*Step #2 Key Terms: *Believe, help, hope, insanity, power, sanity*
*Step #2 Chant:

I'm mad at **you.**	*I'm mad at* **me!**	*I'm mad at my* **insanity!**
It must be **you.**	*It can't be* **me!**	*It's* **not** *my fault, as you can see.*
Help *and* **Hope**	**Help** *and* **Hope**	*By myself, I cannot cope.*

*Review Step #1
I.   I _____ that I was _____ over my _____-
       that my life had become _____.

2.   Why is **honesty** essential if I am going make progress in my recovery?
       _____
       _____

3.   I am **powerless!** My life is **unmanageable!** I can't fix **me!**
       I need **help!**   Why? _____
       I need **hope!**   Why? _____

*Step #2 Introduction: What has your addiction cost you?
1.   I **admit** I have a **hole**, *void,* in my **heart.**
              *What are the **underlying causes** of my heart-hurts?*
              *
              *

2.   I came to believe in my **heart** that there is **help** available.
              *Why do I want **help**?*

3.   There is a Power greater than myself who is available - *ready, willing, and able -*
       to **help** me if I **honestly** admit that I want **help.**
              How can I find this Higher Power?

4.   When I admit I need **help**, there is **hope.** I have hope that my **sanity** can be
       restored, belief that I can have a *normal* life, and trust that something good is
       going to happen to me.
              *How do I know there is **hope** for me?*

5.   What is **sanity**?

6.   What is **insanity**?

7.   What were/are signs of **insanity** in my life?
        *   *
        *   *

8.   What was/is the **pain** of living **with** drugs?

9.   What was/is the **pain** of living **without** drugs?

10.   I choose my addiction **over**:
        *   *
        *   *

11.   My addiction has **cost** me:
        *   *
        *   *

12.   Share a story of **someone** you know who has the same or a similar addiction who
        is now **in recovery**. How does this story provide **hope** for you?

My Personal Higher Power (PHP): The Who or What that Controls Me

1.   **Who** or **what** was the **PHP** that controlled your life **before** you came to
        jail/prison?

2.   What are some reasons you might need a **different** PHP?
        *
        *

3.   Why should you look for a power that is **greater than yourself** and **greater than
        your addiction**?

4.   How could a **new PHP** restore you to **sanity**?

Opportunity knocks! Now is the time for you to **search** for your very own **PHP**. To help you in this unique adventure, you'll want to carefully consider the **qualities you want** in your PHP. You'll also want to look at what **you can do** for your **PHP**.

1.   **Characteristics:** *I want my Higher Power to be:*

      *Loving (example)   *_____   *_____
      *_____   *_____   *_____

2.   **Actions:** *I want my Higher Power to:*

      * Listen (example)   *_____   *_____
      *_____   *_____   *_____

3.   **My Actions:** *I will _____ my Higher Power.*

      *Obey (example)   *_____   *_____
      *_____   *_____   *_____

*Step # 2 Memory Verse: *Luke 15: 17-18 (p. 1318)*
           *When he **finally** came to his **senses**, he said,*
           *I will go **home** to my **father**.*

1.   When **I** finally came to **my** senses, I said, _____
_____

2.   I have practiced writing this verse on the margins of this page and other pages in the homework _____ times and know this verse from memory. _____
                                                      Signature

*Step #2 Extra Credit Verse: *Proverbs 3: 5-6 (p. 789)*   *Draw:*
           Trust *in the Lord with ALL your **heart**;*   **Whole Heart*
           *do NOT depend on your own **understanding**.*   **Head*
           Seek *His will in ALL you do,*   **You*
           *and He will **show** you which **path** to take.*   **Path*

*What happens when you trust in the Lord *half-heartedly?* _____
_____

*What happens when you depend on your own brain to make decisions? _____
_____

*What happens when you don't ask God and don't listen to His opinion before making decisions? _____

 *What different path will you take with God as your boss? _____
_____

2.   I have practiced writing this verse on the margins of this page and other pages in the homework _____ times and know this verse from memory. _____
                                                      Signature

*Step #2 Bible Stories: **A Parable Trilogy-Luke 15**
                                    The Lost Sheep; The Lost Coin; The Lost Son
*Introduction   *Luke 15: 1-2 (pp. 1317)*
1.   Jesus primary method of teaching was with stories *(parables)*.
        Why are stories a good way to teach?

2.   Who were the people that Jesus was eating with and to whom the Pharisees
        objected?

3.   If you invited Jesus to visit and eat with you in jail/prison, would He come? _____
        Why? _____

*Sheep: Lost; Found; Rejoice Over 1%   *Luke 15:3-7 (pp. 1317-18)*
        (appeals to men who were shepherds)
1.   How do you suppose the sheep got lost?

2.   Who searched diligently for the lost sheep?

3.   When the sheep was found, who rejoiced?
        On earth?   In heaven?

4.   Share a time when you got lost due to your own foolishness.

*Coin: Lost; Found; Rejoice Over 10%   *Luke 15:8-10 (p. 1318)*
        (appeals to women who could lose wedding headband coin or a wedding ring)
1.   How do you suppose the coin got lost?

2.   Who searched diligently for the lost coin?

3.   When the coin was found, who rejoiced:
        On earth?   In heaven?

4.   Share a time when you were careless with something of value.

*The Prodigal Son: Lost; Found; Rejoice Over 50%   *Luke 15: 11-24 (p. 1318)*
The Greatest Short Story Ever Told *(In Greek "prodigal" means wasteful)*

Scene #1 (vs. 11-12)   **Rebelling**   **Sick of Home**
1.   Why did the younger son decide to leave home?

2.   What were some characteristics of the younger son at the beginning of the story?
        *
        *

3.   Share a time when you left home with no regard for family and friends' feelings.

Scene #2 (vs. 13-16)   **Reveling**   **Lost Home**

1.   What kind of lifestyle did the son have when he first left home?

2.   Why did the son have lots of friends in this new lifestyle?

3.   When the son was down-and-out, *lost,* why didn't his *frenemies* help him?

4.   To a Jew, the pig was an unclean animal. Jews didn't use pigs as sacrifices, and they didn't eat pork. Once he was *homeless, helpless, and hopeless* describe the son's occupation?

5.   If he had played the *"blame game,"* from the son's point-of-view, whose fault could it have been that he lost all his money and ended up in a pigpen, and why might he have blamed him/them?

Who?	*Why was it his/their fault?*
* father	*
*brother	*
*friends	*
*society	*
*God	*

Scene #3 (vs. 17-19)   **Repenting**   **Homesick**

1.   How do you know that the prodigal son had hit rock bottom and had an *attitude adjustment? (Step #1)*
        *
        *

2.   When the prodigal son came to his senses, he **repented**: *changed his head, his heart, and his direction.* Why did going home to his father make sense to the Prodigal Son?

3.   Why would going home to my heavenly Father make sense for me?
        (lost but not a lost cause; spent everything/had nothing)

Scene #4 (vs. 20-24)   **Restoring**   **Home at Last**

1.   What was the father's reaction when he saw his son coming up the road?

2.   What did the father have the servants get for the son?
        What: *Why:*
        *
        *
        *

3.   Who will celebrate with you in your new life?

4.   As a result of his attitude adjustment, the prodigal son **repented**: *changed his head, his heart, and his direction* - made a U-turn, and went back to his father. What did the father mean when he said, *"For this son of mine was dead, and has now returned to life. He was lost, but now he is found?"*
*

The prodigal son's new motto is, "I can! I will!! I'll obey You!!!
Application: I Rebelled, Repented, Returned, Rejoiced
                    Example from my life:
I disagreed with God. _____
I said, "I want what I want." _____
I ran away from God, _____
I traveled Wild Way Road. _____
I hung out with frenemies. _____
My money ran out. _____
My sanity suffered. _____
I ended up in a pigpen. _____
I was powerless. _____
My life was unmanageable. _____
I finally came to my senses. _____
I went home to my Father (God). _____
I was dead. Now I am alive. _____
Now I know where I belong. _____

6.   What are the characteristics of God found in Jonah 4: 2 *(p. 1139)*:
      God is: *Why is this characteristic important to me?*
      * _____   * _____
      * _____   * _____
      * _____   * _____
      * _____   * _____

*Step #2: Did You Get It?

Please circle True or False, and **explain why** you made each choice.

NA Information *(based on pp. 22-24)*
1.   When I choose to continue to use, this is a sign of insanity.   True   False

2.   If I choose to continue to use, I will end up in prison, or an institution, or a cemetery.   True   False

3.   Guidelines for choosing my Personal Higher Power should include: loving, caring, and greater than myself.   True   False

4.   Without drugs I experience pain, and I am willing to get relief from this pain anyway I can.   True   False
      → **AA Big Book** *(based on Chapter 4: We Agnostics pp. 44-57 and p. 60)*

1.   I may not fully comprehend my Higher Power, but I trust that
     He will help me overcome my addiction.   True   False

2.   My concept of God will have no impact on how I live.   True   False

3.   Hundreds say that God is the most important presence in their
     lives; this is a powerful reason for considering God as my PHP.   T rue   False

12/12 Information *(based on pp. 25-33)*

1.   I often tell God what His will for me should be.   True   False

2.   God will give me what I want if I pray hard enough.   True   False

3.   God can and will restore my sanity if I ask.   True   False

4.   The following are some common attitudes toward God.

     (a)   *"Don't/Won't"* has the attitude, *"You can't make me believe!
           The Bible is full of nonsense."*
     (b)   *"Did/Don't"* has the attitude, *"I used to believe, but God has failed to
           fulfill my demands. I don't believe in Him anymore."*
     (c)   *"Can't"* has the attitude, *"This God stuff is crazy and doesn't make any
           sense."*
     (d)   A *"Want to/Will"* has the attitude, *"As a result of a transformation,
           I came to believe in a Higher Power and began to call Him God."*

*Which of the above attitudes do you have? _____
*Why? _____

5.   The following are labels that might represent you spiritually.

     (a)   **Agnostic**-claims there is no proof for God's existence
     (b)   **Atheist**-claims there is proof that God doesn't exist
     (c)   **Believer**-claims God's existence is based on faith and trust

*Which of the above labels describes you? _____
*Why? _____

6.   What does the Bible say about believing in God? *(Hint: see Psalm 14: 1 (p. 687)*
     Only _____ say in their hearts, "There is no _____."

*Step #2 Reflections:

1.   The prodigal son's poem:

> When **_the prodigal son_** *came to his senses, he screamed, "Oh no!"*
>
> *Rebellion took me farther than I wanted to go!*
>
> *Disobedience made me stay longer than I wanted to stay!*
> *Sin cost me more than I wanted to pay!*   (idea Roland Smith sermon)

My personal poem:

> *When I **came to my senses**, I screamed, "Oh no!"*
> _____ *took me farther than I wanted to go!*
> _____ *made me stay longer than I wanted to stay!*
> _____ *cost me more than I wanted to pay!*

2.   **The prodigal son learned/I learned**
The more he <u>did</u> what he <u>liked</u>
*The less he _____what he _____ *(swap places for underlined words)*
*Was this true in your past life? _____
*Explain your answer: _____

3.   Who did you share Step #2 & *The Prodigal Son Story* with _____
Reactions? _____

4.   **Where I'm Going:** List 3 **new goals** you have for your life when you are released from jail/prison and steps you are going to take to reach these goals?

Goals: *Steps to reach goals:*

●   *

●   *

●   *

Please complete the following check sheet during the week:

Name _____   _____ Class
Dates: _____   _____ Brought Bible/Pencil
Class/Church Attendance   _____ Brought Extra Credit
<u>Date:</u>   <u>Class/Church Name:</u>   _____ Brought Journal

_____   _____
_____   _____   Memory Practice Step #2
_____   _____   _____ Step # 2
_____   _____   _____ Memory Verse
_____   _____   _____ Extra Cr. Memory Verse

Devotions begin on p. 651	Bible Reading	Homework for Step # 2
_____ Devotional #1	_____ Day #1	_____ Day #1
_____ Devotional #2	_____ Day #2	_____ Day #2
_____ Devotional #3	_____ Day #3	_____ Day #3
_____ Devotional #4	_____ Day #4	_____ Day #4
_____ Devotional #5	_____ Day #5	_____ Day #5
_____ Devotional #6	_____ Day #6	_____ Day #6
_____ Devotional #7	_____ Day #7	_____ Day #7

Please write your prayer requests below:

STTA: **Letters to God**

From: 310 Sinners Circle   Lost, TN 38555   April 2013
To: Heavenly Father   7 Redemption Rd.   Agape, Heaven 7077

Dear Lord,
It seems like it always comes to this. It takes my life falling apart in order for me to hit my knees for you. I have made so many mistakes, and now I am facing the consequences of them. I want to move forward from this and not wallow in the pain, pain that I have inflicted upon myself. I make the mess, and then I beg you to pull me out. I know that's not how you work, and I know that you are here with me through these consequences. I just need to remember You are there waiting patiently on me in every moment of my life. Thank you for loving me when I can barely stand myself.
And thank You for the amazing family you have blessed me with. They also love me more than I deserve.   *Love, P. I.*

To: God   Paradise Lane   Heaven

Dear God,
I am so sorry for how I have been living my life. I know I am a big disappointment to you. I have hit the bottom and am ready to start my climb back to the top. I know I can't do this alone and will need your strength and guidance along the way. Please help me find my way back to you, Father. Please help me - a lonely & broken girl to find my way back to the path I need to be on.

I want to thank you for being kind, merciful, loving, forgiving, and understanding.
I know you have never turned away from me, even as many times as I have you.
I probably don't deserve another chance, but I know you will give me one, and for that I will be forever grateful.

I ask that you will help me control my life better and keep the powers of Satan away. I hope to learn the RIGHT way again - your way. Lastly, thank you for yet another chance.   *Love, A. V.*

Dear God,
This is your daughter, H. B. I have prayed to you constantly, and you have helped me through my darkest days. You have given me strength to get through each day as you promised. I am doing my best to live my life as you would want me to. I want to thank you for everything you have done for me, most of all for my sobriety, and for showing me your love. You have given me four beautiful children. Now I will ask one more thing from you! Give me the knowledge to know your will for me and the strength to carry out your will. Fill me with your Holy Spirit and use me to help others. Let me be your servant. I want to do good.
          With all my love, heart, soul, mind, body, and spirit! (H. B.) your Daughter

Rejoice in Recovery 12-Step Faith-Based Study
Participant's Lesson
Step # 3   Date _____
"For I know the plans I have for you," says the Lord.
"They are plans for good and not for disaster, to give you a future and a hope."
Jeremiah 29:11

*Step #3 Smart Start:
*Step # 3   I'll let Him!   *Devotionals start on page 203 LR Bible*
We made a decision to turn our _____ and our _____
over to the care of _____ .

*Step #3 Advice: *Do you want to die? If you want to die, STOP HERE!*
                                        If you want to live, GO ON!
*Step #3 Key Terms: *choice, decision, haphazardly, vacillate, will, will power*
*Step #3 Chant: *I will win! (2X)   I will win, if I let God in!*
                                      I'll decide! (2X)   If in God's care, I will abide.

*Step Review
1.   The 12/12 reminds us that Steps #1 and #2 are **acceptance** steps. Step #3 is an
        affirmative action step. See for yourself by checking the wording for each step.

Step #1: I must **accept** that: _____
_____
Step #2: I must **accept** that: _____
_____
Step #3: I must take the following **affirmative action**: _____
_____

*Step #3 Introduction: What would Jesus do? *(WWJD)*
A wise **decision** is a **choice** that is made deliberately after careful consideration and
evaluation of a number of available options as well as the consequences for each option.
1.   Share **good decisions** you made and **kept**. What were the consequences?
        Decision: *Consequence:*
        *   *

        *   *

2.   Share **good decisions** you made but **didn't keep**.   What were the consequences?
        Decision: *Consequence:*
        *   *

        *   *

3.   Share **bad decisions** you made and **kept**. What were the consequences?
        Decision: *Consequence:*
        *   *

        *   *

4.   Share **bad decisions** you made and **didn't keep**. What were the consequences?
      Decision: *Consequence:*
      *   *

      *   *

5.   Sometimes you make decisions **haphazardly**, *in a disorganized, not well-thought-out manner.* Often the consequences are disastrous. Share a decision you made haphazardly.

6.   When making a decision, often you **vacillate** back and forth between options and find that it's difficult, as Dr. Seuss (1990) points out, *"for a mind-maker-upper to make up his mind."* Share a decision in which you struggled to make up your mind.

7.   My **will** is my *want to.* Often I admit, "I want what I want when I want it, and I want it now!" When my will takes over my life, I often **self-sabotage** myself. I lose control, and as AA says, my *self-will runs riot.* When I am the one in control of me, I often make disastrous decisions. Give an example:
      *

Willpower is *a combination of self-determination and self-discipline that enables me to do something despite the difficulties involved.* I will have to use all of my willpower to turn my **will** and my **life** over to the **care of God** remembering that *where there's a will, there's a way, and where there's no will, there's no way.*

8.   How do you think your life will be different if you make a decision to turn control of your will and your life over to God and make choices based on what **God wants** for you and not on what you want for you?

9.   What do you think will happen to you if God is **not** in control of your decisions?

10.   What are some situations in your life, where what you want differs from God wants for you?
      *
      *

11.   Why is it difficult to turn your **will** over to the care of God*?*

12.   If you turn your **will** and your **life** over to the care of God, what **changes** do you think God will make in your life?
      *
      *

13.   In the past what happened when each of the following controlled your **decisions**?

Controller: *Consequences:*
*Myself   *

*My addiction   *

*My *frenemies*   *

* Step #3 Memory Verse:

For God loves the world so much   *For **God** loved **ME** so much*
that He gave His one and only Son,   *that He gave His one and only **Son**.*
so that everyone who believes in Him   ***If** I trust in Him*
will not perish   ***then** I will not perish*
but have eternal life.   ***but** I will have eternal life.*
John 3:16 NLT (p. 1344)   *John 3: 16 (modified/personalized)*

1.   What can Jesus do for you that you can not do for yourself? _____

_____

2.   I have practiced writing this verse on the margins of this page and other pages in
the homework _____times and know this verse from memory. _____
                                                                      Signature

*Step #3 Extra Credit Verse: *Romans 10: 9 (p. 1445)*   *Draw:*
*If you confess with your **mouth** that Jesus is Lord and*   *You being*
*believe in your **heart** that God raised Him from the dead,*   *saved*
*you will be **saved**.*
1.   Why would you want to be saved? _____

_____

2.   I have practiced writing this verse on the margins of this page and other pages in
the homework _____times and know this verse from memory. _____
                                                                      Signature

*Step #3 Bible Story: Paul: A Man of Dedication, Determination, and Decisions
Saul's Conversion: Acts 9: 1-19 *(pp. 1393-1395)*
**Saul's conversion appears 2 more times in Acts 22 (p. 1417+) & Acts 26 (p. 1422+)
**Saul's name was changed to Paul, Acts 13: 9 (p. 1401)
**Paul's Profile (p. 1401)

1.   Why did Saul *(Paul)* make a decision to go to Damascus, 150 miles from
        Jerusalem?

2.   What kind of an **attention intervention**, *Stop! Look! Listen! Choose-to-Change*
        Experience, did God use to get Saul's *(Paul's)* attention?

3.   What did Saul *(Paul)* ask?   _____
        What was the response?   _____
4.   What did the voice tell Saul *(Paul)* to do?

*
*

5.   What happened when Saul *(Paul)* opened his eyes?
        *
        *

6.   What did Saul *(Paul)* do when he got to Damascus and for how long?

7.   What was Ananias' initial response when the Lord told him to go see Saul *(Paul)*?

8.   What are some things **God wants** you to do, but **you don't want** to do them.
        *
        *
        *

9.   What are some things **God doesn't want** you to do, but **you do** them anyway.
        *
        *
        *

10.   What happened to Saul *(Paul)* after Ananias arrived? *(Hint: see Acts 22: 10 p. 1418)*
        *
        *
        *

11.   Why might Saul *(Paul)* be considered a *basket case*? *(Hint: see Acts 9: 25 p. 1394)*

*Bible Application: Old Friends and New Friends Acts 9: 20-31 *(p. 1394+)*

1.   What are some blind spots in your life?   How could God get your attention?
        *   *

        *   *

        *   *

2.   Give examples of when you were **convinced** that you were totally, utterly, and
        absolutely **right**, and yet you were totally, utterly, and absolutely **wrong**:
        *

        *

        *

3.   Why did Saul *(Paul)* have problems with his **old** friends, the Jews, after he became a Christian? *Hint: See Acts 9: 20-31 and footnote 9: 20-25 (p. 1394)*

4.   Why did Saul *(Paul)* have problems making **new** friends with Christians? *Hint: see Acts 9: 20-31 and footnote 9: 26-30 (p. 1394)*
        *

        *

5.   When Saul *(Paul)* got back to Jerusalem, who came alongside Saul *(Paul)* to sponsor, defend, and encourage him? _____

6.   Why should you make a decision to get a **sponsor** and a **new support group**?

7.   As part of your recovery experience, when you make a **decision** to give up your addictions, what problems are **you** going to have with your **old** friends?
        *

        *

        *

8.   What problems are **you** going to have making **new** friends?
        *

        *

        *

9.   What changes occurred in Saul's *(Paul's)* life after he made a **decision** to accept Christ as his personal Savior?
        *

        *

        *

10.   **Saul/Paul's Story**   **My Story**   **Draw**

A-Accepts____ Jesus as **SAVIOR**.   I Accept _____   *(Brain)*_____

C-Confesses__ his sins and repents.   I Confess _____   *(Mouth)* _____

T-Turns____   his life around.   God Turns _____   *(Body)* _____

S-Surrenders   his **will** and **life** to Jesus   I Surrender _____   *(Heart)* _____
                   as LORD, **BOSS**, of his life.

*Paul and Silas in Prison: Free at Last   **Acts 16: 16-40** *(pp. 1407-1408)*

1.   What decision did Paul and Silas make that upset some wealthy people?

2.   What happened to Paul and Silas as a result of mob violence?
         *

         *

         *

3.   What activities did Paul and Silas **decide** to participate in while in prison?
         *

         *

         Providing positive influence

4.   While in jail/prison, what activities have you made a **decision** to participate in?

5.   What are others learning from you?

6.   What happened as the result of a massive earthquake?
         *

         *

         *

7.   Suppose the doors to your jail/prison flew open, what **decisions** would you make?
         *

         *

8.   The jailer was ready to kill himself, because he feared that all the prisoners had escaped, and that he would be killed. Why did he change his mind?

9.   *What significant question did the jailer ask Paul? _____
         *What was Paul's answer to the question? _____
         *What was the jailer's response? _____

*Step #3: Did You Get It?

Please circle True or False, and **explain why** you made each choice:
Based on: 12/12 Reminders; NA Thoughts; AA Suggestions; Beattie Annotations

1. The whole 12-step program in my life is built on my **willingness**
   to turn my **will** and **life** over to the **care of God**. I am ready,
   willing, and able to do this?   True   False

2. I will pray that God agrees with my will.   True   False

3. I am not under bondage to my addictions.   True   False

4. There is a welcome sense of relief in letting go and letting
   God help me develop a life that is worth living.   True   False

5. There are going to be times when I should take back control of
   my **will** and **life**.   True   False

6. I need relief from **bondage** to myself.   True   False

7. In this step, I need to make a **decision** to live my life differently.   True   False

8. I fear being **abandoned**, and therefore I'm very concerned about
   another person's opinion of me.   True   False

9. One of my biggest problems has been the **misuse** of **willpower**.
   I have tried to handle my problems all by myself.   True   False

10. I agree with the quote below.   True   False

"Our **lives** and our **wills** belong to God. People from our past may have abandoned us. God won't.
When times get rough, we don't have to wonder whether God is there or whether God cares or
whether God knows what is going on. God is there. God cares. God's plan is one we can participate in,
one that lets us use each event and circumstance in our lives to bring about our highest good."
(Melody Beattie, 1990, p. 56)

*Step #3 Reflections:

1. What are you **willing** to let God control?   What changes will God make?
   What: *Change:*
   *   *
   *   *

2. What are you dragging your feet about, because you are **unwilling** to let God
   have control and why?
   What: *Why:*
   *   *

   *   *

3. Who did you share Step #3 and Paul's story with? _____
   Reactions? _____

My Personal Story

Let's suppose that when I leave class today, I go out, get in my car, and head home. As I pull out onto Main Street, a drunk driver slams into my car. I scream! Metal crunches! Glass flies! Sirens wail! Paramedics race; pull me from the wreckage; pronounce me dead at the scene.

A hearse arrives; takes me to the funeral home. My family comes, identifies my body, cries, leaves. Due to the lateness of the hour, the morticians decide to wait until morning to prepare my body for burial.

Later that evening, Jesus comes. "Margie, you're dead. Your life here on earth is over. BUT, have I got a deal for you! I will give you a **new** life, IF you will promise to obey me and do anything I ask you to do."

Anything? Let me think about this. Do I trust You enough to do anything You ask me to do? What are my choices? What are the consequences? Right now, I'm dead. I certainly didn't choose to be dead. BUT, the consequence of that drunk driver's bad decision is that I am absolutely, unequivocally, unintentionally dead. Hm…on the other hand, you're giving me a second chance. IF I choose life, then the consequence of this choice is that I have to forever and ever obey you. Seems like a no-brainer. Life or death?
I choose life, a **new** life with You.

As I sit up, I realize I'm alive! I've been **born again**! I've **made a decision to turn my will and my life over to the care of God**. From now on, no matter what decision I have to make, I must act based on the answer to the question, "What would Jesus do?" I must be **willing** to **go** where Jesus tells me to go, **do** what Jesus tells me to do, and **be** what Jesus tells me to be. I no longer belong to myself. I'm living on borrowed time-Jesus' time *(based on Keith Phillips' story in* The Making of a Disciple. *1981; pp. 18-19).*

The fallacy in this story is that once I die a physical death, I will NOT have a second chance to choose life or death. However, while I am **alive**, I can and must make the **decision** about whether I want to **accept** the opportunity to have a brand-new spiritual life and be **born again** or whether I want to **reject** Jesus.
I am circling the choice I am making:

Decision #1:	**Decision #2:**
Born Twice: Physically and Spiritually	Born Once: Physically
Die Once: Physically	Die Twice: Physically and Spiritually

I am making this decision because _____

Please complete the following check sheet during the week:

Name _____
Dates: _____
Class/Church Attendance
Date: Class/Church Name:

_____   _____
_____   _____
_____   _____
_____   _____
_____   _____

_____ Class
_____ Brought Bible/Pencil
_____ Brought Extra Credit
_____ Brought Journal

Memory Practice Step #3
_____ Step # 7
_____ Memory Verse
_____ Extra Cr. Memory Verse

Devotions begin on p. 203	Bible Reading	Homework for Step # 3
_____ Devotional #1	_____ Day #1	_____ Day #1
_____ Devotional #2	_____ Day #2	_____ Day #2
_____ Devotional #3	_____ Day #3	_____ Day #3
_____ Devotional #4	_____ Day #4	_____ Day #4
_____ Devotional #5	_____ Day #5	_____ Day #5
_____ Devotional #6	_____ Day #6	_____ Day #6
_____ Devotional #7	_____ Day #7	_____ Day #7

Please write your prayer requests below:

STTA: Set Free

Redemption

Are you there or am I dreaming?
Do you hear my cries? My screaming?
Don't you see my spirit straining?
The smoke cloud of my fire draining.

My hope is gone. My strength - it's spent.
My sense of reality, fully bent.
I need You close. I need You near.
Wake up. Listen! Aren't you aware?

They've worked me down, and my heart's
grown cold.
I've lost my soul. I fear it's sold.
Surrounding chaos has left me dazed.
Simply put, I am amazed.

Help me! Save me! Touch me! Hold me!
Restore me back into the old me.
I'm no fool. It won't be easy.
But you have the tools in which to ease me.

You have always calmed my fear and doubt.
You're the love, the peace I can't live without.
I pray you'll answer. I pray you'll hear.
Don't let me suffer. Don't leave me here.

Lost without you, lost in space.
Floating, drifting in this place.
With faith I'll hold onto your rescue.
I'll trust that you will make me brand new.

Holding tight, I won't let go.
In your redeeming grace, my hold will grow.
My heart will sing. My joy will reign.
In your steps, my serenity is what I'll gain.

I'll be your shadow as I follow you.
Convinced your ways are tried and true.
Now basking in my transformation.
Thank you, God, for my creation.
          B. T. 12/10/12
          Submitted to prison ministries for poetry contest

Dear God,

I used to feel so sad inside,
As lonely as could be,
Then you came into my life;
You came to set me free.

Peace, warmth, joy, and love
Are the gifts you gave to me.
Now I stand, blessed from above
For all eternity!

So when I say, "I'll follow you."
It comes from deep within.
I'm ready for a brand new path,
A life that's free of sin.

I want to learn; I want to grow
From all that you can teach.
I yearn to be a part of all
The wisdom that you preach.

In the end, I know you know
That what I say is true.
In my heart is where it lies
Right by my piece of YOU!

                    Love,
                    B. T.

Rejoice in Recovery 12-Step Faith-Based Study
Participant's Lesson
Step # 4   Date _____
"For I know the plans I have for you," says the Lord.
"They are plans for good and not for disaster, to give you a future and a hope."
Jeremiah 29:11

*Step #4 Smart Start:
*Step #4   In-depth inventory   *Devotionals start on page p. 9 LR Bible*
We made a searching and fearless _____ _____ of ourselves.

*Step #4 Paraphrase: *Write about how I got where I am.*
*Step #4 Key Terms: *denial, fear, guilt, inventory, moral, resentment, shame*
*Step #4 Chant: *What's inside? (2X)   What's inside that I want to hide?*
                    Make a list! Check it twice! The good, the bad, the not-so-nice.

*Step #4 Introduction: ***A Journey of Self-Discovery Poem***
*When I take a good, hard, honest **look** at **me**, what do I **see**?*
*This is a journey of **self-discovery**!*
*First, I must **confess**,*
*That my life is an awful **mess.***

1.   **Mentally:** *my boggled brain makes choices that are **senseless**.*
      For example:

2.   **Emotionally:** *my heart feels resentment and **bitterness**.*
      For example:

3.   **Socially:** *I hang out with "frenemies," bad influences on **me**.*
      For example:

4.   **Spiritually:** *I DON'T cry out to God during my **insanity**.*
      For example:

*Then: I Stop! Look! Evaluate! List: what's **right** about **me**?*
*What's **wrong** is a list that is really **scary**!*

5.   What's right about me: What's wrong about me:
            Beauty   *Beast*
*   *

*   *

*   *

*   *

*   *

Barfs: King Solomon said, *"As a dog returns to its vomit (barfs), so a fool repeats his foolishness,"* *(Proverbs 26: 11, p. 815)* Am I a fool? While examining my life, I discover a compulsion to **repeat** the same mistakes over and over and over.

Give examples from your own life for the following key AA/NA terms:

*<u>B</u>itterness is resentment, holding a grudge, and not letting go of bad memories, pent up feelings of insult and injury from the past.

*Who or what stimulates **bitterness** in my life?*	*Why?*
*	*
*	*

*<u>A</u>nger is fury, rage, wrath, being mad, extreme annoyance.

*Who or what stimulates **anger** in my life?*	*Why?*
*	*
*	*

*<u>R</u>ebellion is resisting authority, defiance, going against what's right.

*Who or what stimulates **rebellion** in my life?*	*Why?*
*	*
*	*

*<u>F</u>ear is anxiety over losing what I've got, not getting what I want, or getting caught *(source: anonymous)*; sensing danger, dread, being scared.

*What do I **fear**?*	*Why?*
*	*
*	*

*<u>S</u>elf-Sabotage is destroying myself <u>m</u>entally, <u>e</u>motionally, <u>s</u>ocially, and <u>s</u>piritually.

*How do I **self-sabotage** myself?*	*Why?*
*	*
*	*

With God's guidance you can develop and write a searching and fearless **moral inventory** listing *the good, the bad, and the ugly events* from your past. How can you determine what God's **moral standards** of behavior are?

You could: *Explain the advantages and/or disadvantages of each source:*

*Ask *frenemies* _____

*Ask family _____

*Ask yourself _____

*Ask God _____

*Read your Bible _____

Are you ready, willing, and able, with God's guidance and suggestions from AA/NA, to consider taking a searching and fearless **moral inventory** of your life? If your answer is, *"Yes,"* go on. If your answer is, *"No,"* discuss with God and your sponsor.

*Step #4 Memory Verse: **Draw**
__Search__ me, O God, and know my __heart__;   *Heart being searched:*
__test__ me and know my anxious __thoughts__.   *Brain being tested:*
__Point out__ anything in me that __offends__ You, and   *Problems being pointed out:*
__lead__ me along the __path__ of __everlasting__ life.   *You on path to heaven:*
Psalm 139: 23-24 (p. 776)   *(see The Message Bible)*

1.   What in my heart and mind might offend God? _____

        _____

2.   I have practiced writing this verse on the margins of this page and other pages in
        the homework _____ times and know this verse from memory. _____
                                                                        Signature

*Step #4 Extra Credit Verse: *Psalm 118: 8 (p. 762)*
        It is better to take __refuge__ in the __Lord__ than to __trust__ in __people__.
                (Some people say this is the center verse in the Bible.)

1.   In the past, in whom have you put your trust, why, what happened? _____

        _____

2.   I have practiced writing this verse on the margins of this page and other pages in
        the homework _____ times and know this verse from memory. _____
                                                                        Signature

*Step #4 Bible Stories: **Satan Tempts Adam and Eve**   *(Genesis 3 pp. 7-9)*
                                        Satan Tempts Jesus   *(Matthew 4: 1-11 pp. 1200-1201)*

Scripture Background:
1.   What does **manipulate** mean?

2.   How does Satan try to **manipulate** you?

*

*

*

3.   Why do you think AA teaches - we should **not** say, "The devil **made** me do it."

Beginning of Conversation: Satan the Master Manipulator
How did the devil deceive Eve?

<u>D</u>-Doubt *(uncertainty; suspect something is not true)*
1.   How did the devil cause Eve to **doubt**?

        *

2.   How does the devil tempt you to **doubt**? *(Satan-tempts; God tests-James 1: 12+)*
        *

        *

<u>E</u>-Entice *(tempt to do something wrong often through eyes, ears, & emotions)*
3.   How did the devil **entice** Eve?

        *

4.   How does the devil **entice** you?
        *

        *

<u>V</u>-Victim Mentality *(feel taken advantage of; tricked)*
5.   How did the devil make Eve feel like a **victim**?

        *

6.   How does the devil make you feel like a **victim**?
        *

        *

<u>I</u>-Impulsive *(taking action without thinking)*
7.   How did the devil get Eve to act **impulsively**?

        *

8.   How does the devil get you to act **impulsively**?
        *
        *

<u>L</u>-Lies: *(not telling the truth, the whole truth, and nothing but the truth)*
9.   What **lies** did the devil tell Eve?

        *

10.   What **lies** does the devil tell you?
        *
        *

Middle of Conversation: Confrontation & The Blame Game
1.   Why did Adam and Eve hide? Compare to Genesis 2: 25.

2.   God asked Adam, "Have you eaten from the tree whose fruit I commanded you **not** to eat?" How did Adam attempt to evade the question and shift blame?

3.   God asked Eve, "What have you done." How did Eve shift blame?

4.   God asked Adam and Eve the following questions *(see Genesis 3: 9-14)*:
      *
      *
      *
      *

How would you answer the following questions that are similar to the questions God asked Adam and Eve?

      God's question to you: *Your answer to God:*
      *What about your addiction   *
      are you trying to hide from me?

      *What have you done that I told you   *
      not to do?

End of Conversation: Choices and Consequences
The serpent, Adam, Eve, and now you made bad **choices**.
As a result, there were and continue to be **consequences**.

1.   What were the serpent's **consequences** for **bad choices**/sins?

2.   What were Eve's **consequences** for **bad choices**/sins?

3.   What were Adam's **consequences** for **bad choices**/sins?

4.   What are some **bad choices** you've made, and what were/are the **consequences**:
      Choices: *Consequences:*
      *   *

      *   *

      *   *

5. What happened in your life when Satan, referring to your *addiction-of-choice*, enticed you whispering, *"Try It! You'll like it!"*

6. What **might** have happened in your life regarding your addiction if Satan had declared, *"Try it! You'll die from it."*

*Application: Eve's and My Temptations *(Genesis 3)*
Fill in: *How Does Satan Tempt Me Through; *My Responses (Visual: Eyes, Ears, Emotions)

Types of Temptation Satan Used	Satan's Temptations to Eve	Eve's Responses	*How Does Satan Tempt Me Through:	*My Responses
Eyes **If it LOOKS good, grab it!**	Fruit looked delicious.	Took a bite.	Eyes?	
Ears **If it SOUNDS good, listen to it!**	You'll be like God!	Conversation with the devil.	Ears?	
Emotions **If it FEELS good, do it!**	What a deal! Wanted Wisdom.	Shared with Adam. The Great Oops!	Emotions?	

Application: Jesus' and My Temptations *(Matthew 4: 1-11 pp. 1200-1201)*
Fill in: *Satan's Temptations to Jesus; *How Does Satan Tempt Me?
*   *My Out-Loud Scripture Responses (3 different personal verses)*

Types of Temptation Satan Used**	*Satan's Temptations to Jesus	Jesus' Scripture Responses	*How Does Satan Tempt Me?	*My Out-Loud Scripture Responses
Provide for your **physical** needs.		The scriptures say… Deut. 8: 3	What physical temptations do I face?	Write out a personal verse. Include reference.
Take a ridiculous risk. God will rescue you.		The scriptures also say… Deut. 6: 16	What ridiculous risks do I take?	Write out a personal verse. Include reference.
Worship anyone or anything but God.		For the scriptures say… Deut. 6: 13	Who or what do I worship?	Write out a personal verse. Include reference.

**Classification of the types of temptations Jesus experienced is difficult and something about which Bible scholars do not agree. The chart classifications are the author's interpretation.

*Step #4: Did You Get It? *Self-Assessment Inventory: The Good, The Bad, & The Ugly

The Good

Who did I help?	What happened? *Event*	Impact on my attitudes and actions?
* * *	* * *	* * *
Who helped me?	**What happened?** *Event*	**Impact on my attitudes and actions?**
* * *	* * *	* * *

The Bad and The Ugly

Who did I hurt/harm? *Resentful at me*	What happened? *Event*	Impact on my attitudes and actions?
* * *	* * *	* * *
Who hurt/harmed me? *Resentful at*	**What happened?** *Event*	**Impact on my attitudes and actions?**
* * *	* * *	* * *

*Step #4: Reflections:
(based on **AA** *(pp. 64-71)*; **12/12** *(42-53)*; **and NA** *(pp. 27-30)*)
Self-Assessment
Who am I? I must **self-assess**,

Because my life is an awful mess.

    First, I'll write an **inventory**.

    A detailed grudge-list for me to see.

Of whom I've hurt and who's hurt me,

My life-long-ledger of misery.

    To **denial**, I'll call a halt.

    No longer say, "It's not my fault."

Or say, it's not so bad-that's **minimizing**.

It's not hurting others-that's **rationalizing**.

    No more, **justification**, **fabrication**.

    No more, self/other **manipulation**.

No more, "I'll get even with you."

No more, blaming others for what I do.

    No more, excuses for bad behavior,

    I'm taking a stand and will not waver.

With faith in God, I'll have no fear,

My guilty conscious is now clear.

    Others may leave, but God will stay.

    God will be with me all the way.

I've had a complete self-examination.

Now I'm done! Exaltation!

My New Moral Goals:
*

*

*

*

How I will achieve these goals:
*

*

*

Please complete the following check sheet during the week:

Name _____

Dates: _____

Class/Church Attendance

Date: Class/Church Name:

_____   _____

_____   _____

_____   _____

_____   _____

_____   _____

_____ Class

_____ Brought Bible/Pencil

_____ Brought Extra Credit

_____ Brought Journal

_____ Memory Practice Step #4

_____ Step #4

_____ Memory Verse

_____ Extra Cr. Memory Verse

Devotions begin on p. 9	Bible Reading	Homework for Step #4
_____ Devotional #1	_____ Day #1	_____ Day #1
_____ Devotional #2	_____ Day #2	_____ Day #2
_____ Devotional #3	_____ Day #3	_____ Day #3
_____ Devotional #4	_____ Day #4	_____ Day #4
_____ Devotional #5	_____ Day #5	_____ Day #5
_____ Devotional #6	_____ Day #6	_____ Day #6
_____ Devotional #7	_____ Day #7	_____ Day #7

Please write your prayer requests below:

STTA: Journal Entries In-Jail and Out-of-Jail

In-Jail

Mrs. Margie,

I wanted to send a lil note to thank you & the girls *(women's team)* for all ya'll do. The effort ya'll spend coming in here *(jail)* with the message and the lessons can only be appreciated & matched when I do the lessons and "believe" the message. I do believe as I think you clearly see thru my participation & growth over the last months.

I can say your intro into Step 4 is exactly what I needed. I had hesitated & procrastinated in my past on that step. I paid dearly for that error. Now I've had a taste of it, it's not so super bad. Yes it hurts to see all my flaws. However, it didn't kill me! It let me know what I need to work on & that many people struggle with the same issues. We are all imperfect, and I feel that this life is like a battle between good & evil!!

I feel like the Lord will lead my feet to the good. I can see that He is clearing me a cleaner/safer path. I bawl about all the works He's doing in my life & others' lives also. I get the, "I can't. He can. & I'll let Him." *(Steps 1,2, & 3)* these days.

My Lord truly answers prayers, and I see this with different eyes than I had in the past, if that makes sense. I don't know if I understand fully, but I know I'm a baby in my relationship w/Christ. I have much to learn, see, give, and receive. I am very blessed that God never gave up on me. He stood by me when I didn't want to stand anywhere around myself. He didn't throw in the towel when I had at times. His love is unfailing 100%. The love, hope, encouragement, peace and faith is a blessing, miracle, & gift from my God. I know that now anyways.

Thanks for all you do. I love you, *S. W.*

Out-of-Jail Bits-and-Pieces

Week #1

*Today I allowed God to teach me how not to slip back into my old ways when tempted. He showed me that there is always a better way. Just to turn my problems over to him.

*Today I cleaned house and helped move some furniture and made spaghetti for dinner, and I spent some much needed time thinking about the things I need to do differently now that I have a second chance.

*Today I am grateful that God let me wakeup and gave me another day to be a Mom and to spend time on this beautiful earth that he created for us. My grouch for today is - it is raining, and I can't really get outside and do anything. BUT at least I'm NOT in jail and can sit on the porch and watch the rain.

*Today has been very stressful, and BEFORE I would have gone and gotten high. BUT I am a different person today. I got mad and cried, and the thought of getting high never crossed my mind.

Week #2

*I went to the Bread of Life Mission tonight for the meeting, and I am so glad and blessed to have met Mrs. Margie, Sonya, and all the wonderful supportive people there. They are really making a huge difference in my life.

*I woke up and got to have one more day without using drugs! Thank you Lord!

*I have learned not to take anything for granted cause it can all be gone in the blink of an eye.

*I am learning to deal with pain without medication and to be more considerate of others.

*God has taught me that He will be by my side, and that I may not think He hears my prayers, but he does.

*Today I am so thankful that God has given me such loving daughters, wonderful friends, and one more morning to sit on the back porch, drink my coffee, and enjoy everything in my life.

I woke up with my daughters in the bed with me. It's a beautiful day, and I plan on making the most of it. *(K. M.)*

Rejoice in Recovery 12-Step Faith-Based Study
Participant's Lesson
Step #5   Date _____
"For I know the plans I have for you," says the Lord.
"They are plans for good and not for disaster, to give you a future and a hope."
Jeremiah 29: 11

*Step #5 Smart Start:
*Step #5:   **Admit 3.**   *Devotionals start on page 59 LR Bible*
        We _____ to _____, to _____, and to _____
        the exact nature of our wrongs.
*Step #5 Paraphrase: *Tell another person all of my private, embarrassing secrets.*
                                   Let God listen. Sharing hurts helps.
*Step #5 Key Terms: *admit; exact nature; nightmares; thorough; transparent*

*Step #5 Chant: *Share with **God**. Share with **you**. Share my secrets with **me** too.*
                          Honesty! Honesty! Is what God expects from me.

*Step #5 Introduction: Is there a nightmare in your closet?
                    (The following is based on AA; 12/12; NA)
1.   Get ready to share your Step 4 personal moral inventory that includes *the good;*
the bad; and the ugly in your life including those you've *helped, harmed,* and *hurt.*
        Draw a **seating plan** for your sharing session. On this plan draw 3 chairs with a
name on each chair for those who will be involved in your *admit-session (check step*
wording).

When sharing the ***exact*** *nature of your wrongs*, what you share must pass the
3-T Test - each explanation for the mistakes you've made must be:
        Thorough: complete including each and every detail, leaving nothing out
        Truthful: honest, accurate
        Transparent: crystal clear explanation; **not** *talking-in-circles* in order to confuse
        the listener and cloud the issue

2.   **Thorough:** Share an example of a time when you made a mistake, admitted the
        mistake to someone else, **but** decided to **leave out** some of the *down and dirty*
        details (sin of omission).

3.   **Truthful:** Share an example of a time when you made a mistake, admitted the
        mistake to someone else, **but** decided to be *less-than-truthful* in your
        explanation.

4.   **Transparent:** Share an example of a time when you made a mistake, admitted
        the mistake to someone else, **but** decided to *talk-in-circles* hoping to confuse the
        listener.

5.   Why should I share my take-with-me-to-the-grave secrets, *the nightmares in my closet,* with **God**? He already knows what I have done.
*
*
*

6.   According to Psalm 32 *(LRB p. 700),* what are the advantages of confessing your sins to God?

*	*
*	*
*	*

7.   According to Psalm 32 what are the disadvantages of NOT confessing your sins to God?

*	*
*	*

8.   Why should I share my secrets, *the nightmares in my closet,* with **myself**, after all I already know my own deep, dark secrets?
*
*
*

9.   Suppose you were to sit down in front of a large mirror, look at yourself, and read out loud your Step 4 personal moral inventory that includes *the good; the bad; and the ugly* in your life including those you've *helped, harmed,* and *hurt.* What do you think your reactions would be? *(Hint: check out James 1: 22-25, p. 1601)*
*
*

10.   Why should I share my secrets with **another human being**? My secrets are nobody else's business.
*

*

*

11.   What qualifications should the person I'm going to share my secrets with have?
*
*
*

12.   With whom should I **not** share my secrets?

*Step #5 Memory Verse
>   But if we **_confess_** our **_sins_** to **_Him_**,
>   He is **_faithful_** and **_just_** to **_forgive_** us our sins and
>   To **_cleanse_** us from all wickedness. 1 John 1: 9 (p. 1628)

1.   Why should you confess/admit your sins to God? _____
       _____

2.   If you confess your sins to God and then keep doing the same old thing over and
       over again, what changes do you need to make? _____
       _____

3.   I have practiced writing this verse on the margins of this page and other pages in
       the homework _____ times and have memorized it. _____
                                                                                                    Signature

* Step #5 Extra Credit Verse
       *Keep me from **lying** to **myself**;*
       *Give me the **privilege***
       *of knowing your **instructions**. Psalm 119: 29 (p. 764)*

1.   Give examples of when you have lied to yourself: _____
       _____

2.   Why did you tell yourself these lies? _____
       _____

3.   How should you deal with yourself when you lie? _____
       _____

4.   It has been said that, *"A liar should have a good memory."* Why is this a very
       strong argument for not telling a lie? _____
       _____

5.   I have practiced writing this verse on the margins of this page and other pages in
       the homework _____ times and have memorized it. _____
                                                                                                    Signature

*Step #5 Bible Story: David, a Man after God's Own Heart

David Anointed King *1 Samuel 16: 1-13 (p. 365)*
1.   What was Samuel's Task?

2.   What were Eliab's qualifications to be king?

3.   How did God determine who should be the next king?

4.   Why wasn't David in the line-up with his brothers?

5.   What happened to David after he was anointed?

6.   Even though David was the least likely to be anointed king, God chose him. Even
       though you might be the least likely to do a job, why might God choose you?

7.   Since God judges us by our hearts, what are some characteristics our hearts
       should have? Draw a heart, and label with these characteristics. *Hint: Check out
       LRB footnote for 16: 6-13 (p. 365).*

Goliath Challenges the Israelites *1 Samuel 17: 1-31 (p. 366-67)*
1.   Describe Goliath's 4 A's:
      *Appearance:
      *Actions:
      *Attitude:
      *Articulation *(words)*:

2.   What were Saul's and the army's responses to Goliath?

3.   David was too young to be fighting. Why was David visiting the troops?

4.   David checked to see what he'd get for killing Goliath. Share an example of
      when you checked before making a decision to see *what's in it for me.*

David Kills Goliath *1 Samuel 17: 32-51 (pp. 367-68)*
1.   What was Saul's response to David's offer to fight Goliath?

2.   In the past how had God prepared David for his encounter with Goliath?
      *
      *

3.   How did Saul try to prepare David for battle?

4.   How did David prepare for battle?
      *
      *
      *

5.   Why was David able to kill Goliath? *(Hint: lion & bear battles prepare us to fight giants)*
      *
      *
      *

6.   Who/What are some giants in your life? How do you fight them?
      Giants: *Fight how:*
      *   *
      *   *
      *   *

David and Bathsheba *II Samuel 11: 1-13 (p. 400)*
The Great Oops in David's life?
1.   David wasn't where he should have been, out fighting with his troops, and he got
      in trouble. Explain David's:
      *Temptation:
      *Problem:
      *Solution:
2.   Why didn't David's plan to *set-up* Uriah as the father of the baby work?

3.   *Idle hands are the devil's tools* is a well-known saying. David had *time-on-his-hands*, and he got in big trouble. Share a time when you had *time-on-your-hands*, and you got in big trouble.
      *

David a Murderer *II Samuel 11: 14-17 (p. 401)*

1.   What was David's final solution to his problem with Uriah?

2.   What was wrong with David's solution to his problem?

Nathan Rebukes David *II Samuel 12: 1-14 (p. 401)*

1.   Nathan told David a story with the following characters:

Story Characters:	*Real-Life Character:*
*Rich man	*
*Poor Man	*
*Little Lamb	*

      Poor Man:
            *What kind of pet did he have? _____
            *How do you know he loved his pet? _____
            _____

      Rich Man:
            *Characteristics? _____
            *Why did he do what he did? _____
            _____

2.   What was David's initial response to the story? _____
      _____

3.   Nathan *held-up a mirror*, confronted David, and said: _____

4.   Was David able to sin successfully and get away with what he had done? _____
      *Explain your answer: _____
      _____

5.   Can you sin successfully and get away with what you've done? _____
      *Explain your answer: _____
      _____

6.   Then David **confessed** to Nathan,
            *"I have **sinned** against the **Lord**." Nathan replied, "Yes, but the **Lord** has **forgiven** you, and you won't **die** for this sin. 2 Samuel 12: 13 (p. 401)*
      Who suffered the **consequences** of David's sin?
      *
      *
      *

7.   Who has suffered the **consequences** of your secret sins *(character defects; shortcomings)*?

*Application

1.   *How can you: (unknown source)*
*Learn from and let go of the past?   _____

_____

*Live contentedly in the present   _____

_____

*Look forward confidently to the future _____

_____

2.   David said, *"The LORD who rescued me from the claws of the <u>lion</u> and the <u>bear</u>
       will rescue me from <u>this Philistine!</u>" (1 Samuel 18: 37)*
       You might say, *"The LORD who rescued me from the claws of* _____ *and*
       _____*will rescue me from* _____ ."

3.   Realizing that *idle hands are the devil's tools,* how can you avoid this pitfall
       when you get out of jail/prison? *(Hint: how are you going to stay meaningfully
       occupied with good activities?)*
*

*

4.   Psalm 51 was composed by David to express his sorrow and repentance after
Nathan confronted him about his adultery with Bathsheba. In Psalm 51 what are some of
the things David asked God to do for him?

David asked for?	*Why?*
*	*
*	*
*	*
*	*
*	*
*	*

5.   According to Psalm 51, God does NOT want a sacrifice/burn offering.

What does God want from me?	*Why?*
*	*
*	*
*	*

6.   Ecclesiastes 4: 9-12 *(LRB p. 828)* points out beautifully the advantages of 3
       people standing together when being attacked.
       *What is the disadvantage of fighting by yourself? _____

       _____

       *What is the advantage of two standing back-to-back? _____

       _____

       *What is the advantage of adding a third person or God? _____

       _____

*Step #5 Did You Get It?

I've Got a Secret	*Why might I decide to keep my nightmares a secret?*

I've got a secret
Nobody knows.

    The longer I hide it,
    The *worser* it grows.

*

I don't want to see it,
Or look at my face.

*

    If anyone knew,
    I would live in disgrace.

*

To even remember
Brings me great shame,

*

    And my Higher Power,
    Can I claim His name?

I'll hide it from God,
And I'll hide it from you.

What are some advantages of cleaning out my closet and getting rid of my nightmares?

    And I'll never tell,
    Whatever I do.

I'll go to my grave;
My guilt never share.

*

    If it was revealed,
    I would die in despair.

*

Oh God, please forgive me;
I've brought you great shame.

*

    And there is no hope,
    Till I call on your name.

*

I must tell my secret
To **God**, **me**, and **you**,

    Cause my recovery depends
    On beginning anew.

---

4. "We need to tell God about ourselves: quietly, loudly, silently. During our morning meditation, our afternoon break, or our evening walk, we need to say, 'God,

How I would complete each thought:

This is who I am: _____
This is what I did: _____
This is what I think: _____
This is what I want: _____
This is what I need: _____
This is what I'm feeling: _____
This is what I'm going through: _____
This is what I'm worried about: _____
These are my fears, my hopes: _____
These are my old beliefs: _____
This is what I think I can't deal with: _____
This is what I need help with: _____

" Hey, God, this is me." *(p. 93 reformatted; Melody Beattie 1990)*

*Step #5 Reflections:

David	_____ *(My Name)*	*Example from My Life*
Was <u>great kid</u>	* I was <u>great kid</u>	*
Was <u>great guy</u> *(gal)*	* I was <u>great "guy"</u>	*
Then his God he did defy	* Then my God I did defy	*
Had <u>great goof</u>	* I had <u>great goof</u>	*
Caused <u>great grief</u>	* I caused <u>great grief</u>	*
His <u>great God</u> gave relief	* My <u>great God</u> gave relief	*

*Who did you share Step #5 and David's story with? _____
Reactions? _____

*Where I'm Going: Please identify 3 things that you are going to **confess** to God, **ask forgiveness for**, and **eliminate** from your life. What strategies are you going to use to ensure these things do not return?

Confess: *Strategies to eliminate:*

*   *

*   *

*   *

Please complete the following check sheet during the week:

Name _____   _____ Class
Dates: _____   _____ Brought Bible/Pencil
Class/Church Attendance   _____ Brought Extra Credit
<u>Date:</u>   <u>Class/Church Name:</u>   _____ Brought Journal

_____   _____
_____   _____   Memory Practice Step #5
_____   _____   _____ Step #5
_____   _____   _____ Memory Verse
_____   _____   _____ Extra Cr. Memory Verse

Devotions begin on p. 59   Bible Reading   Homework for Step #5
_____ Devotional #1   _____ Day #1   _____ Day #1
_____ Devotional #2   _____ Day #2   _____ Day #2
_____ Devotional #3   _____ Day #3   _____ Day #3
_____ Devotional #4   _____ Day #4   _____ Day #4
_____ Devotional #5   _____ Day #5   _____ Day #5
_____ Devotional #6   _____ Day #6   _____ Day #6
_____ Devotional #7   _____ Day #7   _____ Day #7

Please write your prayer requests below:

STTA: **Poems to Ponder**

So Long

For me, His love was something totally new.
Why it took me **so long**, I haven't a clue.
His love and kindness are so very strong.
Why in the world did it take me so long……
      So long to accept the free love He gives,
      To accept the way He wants me to live.
      He spoke to me often, but I never heard,
      The comfort that was provided in His word.
So long to accept His unconditional love,
To realize I could be an example of…
His glory and even His shining light,
And to help save others from an undesired plight.
      So long to accept His care and nurture,
      As He removed my fears and inner torture.
      He removed all my defects as well as my labels,
      As I allowed Him to touch me, my life became stable.
So long to accept His open and loving arms,
That immediately removed me from any harm.
And to allow Him to offer me an open ear,
So I know my prayers He will always hear.
      So long to accept the fact that He's real;
      To finally realize His acceptance is a BIG DEAL!
      To know that it's only Him that I care to please,
      And to know the importance of hitting my knees!   *(A. B. - January 12, 2013)*

Unchained

My chains are bound, no where to run.
Locked behind these doors, not able to have fun.
I have lost everything: my freedom, my family, and all.
Why Lord, why did I have to fall?
      I sit here and wonder - how could I get free?
      But the Lord tells me, "My dear child, not without me!"
      I still ignore the answers, as I have done before,
      Just like He is talking right to the door…
I feel handcuffs on my wrists, knowing they're not there, and
Shackles on my feet and going nowhere…
I feel like my life has come to an end,
Until someone showed me my true best friend…
      There is no other like Him; I wish you could see,
      He has turned my life around to show the real me.
      I ask for forgiveness. He forgives me again.
      I really want to walk with my new best friend.
My chains no longer bound. I am set free!!
Thank you my Dear Lord for saving me.
I would love to share my best friend with you.
Don't worry; He can be your best friend too… *(J. L. - January 10, 2010)*

Rejoice in Recovery 12-Step Faith-Based Study
Participant's Lesson
Step #6   Date _____
"For I know the plans I have for you," says the Lord.
"They are plans for good and not for disaster, to give you a future and a hope."
Jeremiah 29: 11

*Step #6 Smart Start:
*Step #6:   I surrender!   *Devotionals start on p. 33 LRB*
    We were _____ _____ to have God _____ all these _____.

*Step #6 Paraphrase: *Decide whether or not you want to live your old life anymore*
                    Choice: To change or not to change that is the dilemma
*Step #6 Key Terms: *change, choice, consequence, surrender, transformation*

*Step #6 Chant: *Change or not? Change or not? I must think on this a lot.*
                    Take my hurts! Take my woes! My defects have got to go!

*Step #6 Introduction: Preparation for Transformation: Get Ready! Get Set!

1.   **Surrender** means to turn over control, to let go. In his world-wide best-seller, The Purpose Driven Life, Rick Warren says, *"Everyone eventually **surrenders** to something or someone. You are **free to chose** what to surrender to, **BUT** you are **not free** from the **consequences** of that choice."*
        *What are the **consequences** when you surrender to your addiction?

        *What are the **consequences** when you surrender to God?

2.   List some of your character defects that deal with ***destructive attitudes****: thoughts, emotions, and feelings,* that you are entirely ready and willing, to surrender to God. *(e.g. resentment Hint: see Galatians 5: 19-21 p. 1505)*
        *   *

        *   *

        *   *

3.   List some of your character defects that involve ***destructive actions*** that you are entirely ready and willing, to surrender to God. *(e.g. stealing Hint: see Ten Commandments Exodus 20: 1-17 p. 102+; things God detests Proverbs 6: 16-19 p. 793)*
        *   *

        *   *

        *   *

4.   **I** am **ready**, **willing,** and **able** to change, when I
*Admit I have a problem
*Accept full responsibility for my own faults and failures
*Ask God humbly and sincerely for help in the removal of my destructive habits
I'm going to say, *"Good-bye to the old me! Hello to the new me!"*
Choices I am ready and willing to make: *(Hint: Ephesians 4: 25-32, p. 1514-1515)*
Example:
I am ready and willing to live without *lying*.
I am ready and willing to live with *telling the truth*.

I am ready and willing to live without _____
I am ready and willing to live with _____

I am ready and willing to live without _____
I am ready and willing to live with _____

I am ready and willing to live without _____
I am ready and willing to live with _____

I am ready and willing to live without _____
I am ready and willing to live with _____

I am ready and willing to live without _____
I am ready and willing to live with _____

*Step #6 Memory Verse: *Romans 12: 2 (pp. 1447-1448)*
*Don't **copy** the behavior and customs of this world,*   **Draw changed brain:*
*but **let** God **transform** you into a **new** person*
*by **changing** the way you **think**.*
1.   What happens when you **copy** the behavior and customs of the *addiction world*?

_____
2.   "What's going to **change** in your life when you are entirely ready to let God
transform you? _____
3.   How are you going to **know** what God wants you to do? _____

_____
4.   I have practiced writing this verse on the margins of this page and other pages in
the homework _____ times and know this verse from memory _____
                                                                                                    signature
*Step #6 Extra Credit Verse: *1 Corinthians 6: 19-20 (p. 1463)*
*You do not belong to **yourself**,*   **Draw changed heart:*
*for God bought you with a high **price**,*
*so you must honor God with your **body**.*
1.   How do you honor and dishonor God with your body?
Honor: *Dishonor:*
•   *
•   *
•   *

2.   What is the high price God paid for you? _____
_____

3.   I have practiced writing this verse on the margins of this page and other pages in
the homework _____ times and know this verse from memory. _____
Signature

*Step #6 Bible Story: Moses Moments *Exodus 1-4 (pp. 77-83)*

*Education: 40 Years as a Powerful Prince in a Palace *(@1/3 Life)*
Exodus 1: 22 - 2: 1-10 (p. 79)
1.   How did baby Moses' mother save his life?

2.   How did Moses get to grow up as a powerful prince in a palace?

3.   Application: How did God protect you, or appear not to protect you, when you
were young?

*Preparation for Transformation: 40 Years in the Desert *(@1/3 Life)*
Exodus 2:11-25-3: 1-6 (pp. 79-80) *(Does incarceration provide preparation for transformation?)*
1.   How do you know that Moses wasn't entirely ready to give up his **character
defects**, *destructive attitudes and actions*?

2.   How does Moses attempt to hide, *cover up*, his impulsive *out-of-control temper-
tantrum* choice?

3.   What were the **consequences** of Moses' *out-of-control temper-tantrum* choice?
*

*

4.   Application: Share a time when you made a choice to have an *out-of-control
temper-tantrum* that ended with disastrous results.

**Confrontation: Burning Bush *Exodus 3: 1-6 (p. 80)*
1.   What was amazing about the burning bush Moses saw?

2.   What did God tell Moses to do in Verse 5, and why should he do this?
*What?
*Why?

3.   What was Moses' reaction to God speaking to him?

**Exasperation: God said, *"Now go…"* and Moses demonstrated that he was not entirely ready and willing to surrender to God's will.
Read verses and fill-in-the-chart Exodus 3: 11- 4: 17 (pp. 80-82)

"BUT" Moses Protested/Pleaded *(said; asked)*	God's Answer
#1 (3: 11-12)	
#2 (3: 13-15)	
#3 (4: 1-9)	3 Signs * * *
#4 (4: 10-12)	
#5 (4: 13-17)	

*Application: What are **my excuses** when God asks me to do something I don't want to do?
*
*
*

*Frustration: 40 Years of Irritation, Aggravation, & Agitation

**Ten-Plague-Push *Exodus 7-11 (pp. 86-91)*
1.   What were the 10 Plagues?

1.	*4.*	*7.*	*10.*
2.	*5.*	*8.*	
3.	*6.*	*9.*	

*Application: What kinds of ***tough-love-pushes*** does God give **you** when you don't give Him complete control of your life? (*Hint: LRB footnote Exodus 11: 9-10 p. 91*)

**Egyptian Pursuit; Israelite Escape *Exodus 14 (pp. 95-96)*
1.   The Israelites were boxed in. They panicked. They had the Egyptians behind
        them, and the sea in front of them. They were quick to complain. What did they
        ask Moses?
        *
        *
        *

2.   What were Moses' responses to their rebellion?
        *   *
        *   *

3.   God told Moses to step out in faith and get the people moving.
        What miracle did God perform, so that the people could get through the sea?

4.   Share a time when you rebelled against God, and yet God saved you from
        yourself.

**The Ten Commandments   *Exodus 20: 1-21 (pp. 102-103)*
1.   The first four commandments deal with our relationship to _____
        How did Jesus summarize this relationship?
                (Hint: LRB footnote 20: 1-11; Matthew 22: 37, p. 1232)
        _____

2.   In your life, why is your relationship with God important? _____
        _____

3.   The other six commandments deal with your relationship to _____
        How did Jesus summarize this relationship?
                (Hint: LRB footnote 20: 12-17; Matthew 22: 39, p. 1232)
        _____
        _____

4.   Why does God want you to love **yourself**? _____
        _____

5.   Why should you love yourself as much as you love others? _____
        _____

**The Gold Calf   *Exodus 32: 1-35 (pp. 116-118)*
1.   What was wrong with the people worshiping the gold calf?

2.   What did Moses do with the gold calf?
        *   *
        *   *

3.   Who did Aaron blame for the gold calf in essence saying, *"It's not my fault!"*
        *
        *

4.   Application: what are some *idols, gold calves,* you worshipped in the **past**, your rationalization for this worship, and the consequences of idol-worship?

What? (Idols/calves)   Rationalization/Why?   Consequences?
Example: Meth   *Makes me feel good*   *Arrested; put in jail*

*   *   *

*   *   *

*   *   *

*Step #6: Did You Get It? *(based on AA; 12/12; NA)*
        PLEASE circle True or False, and **EXPLAIN** each answer.

1.   If I ask Him to, God will remove my character defects.   True False

2.   I can remove my character defects all by myself.   True False

3.   I am **not** ready to part with some of my character defects.   True False

4.   I am willing to ask God to help me **want** to part with
        my *favorite* character defects.   True False

5.   My best efforts, along with the help of family and friends,
        will cure my addiction.   True False

6.   God wants a new life for me.   True False

7.   I want a new life for me, or I am going to self-destruct.   True False

8.   When using or abusing (alcohol, drugs, sex, money),
        I am losing. I am slowly committing suicide.   True False

9.   **I want** the reward of changing; I just **don't want** to face
        all the work necessary to change.   True False

10.   Once I hit bottom, my defects caused me excessive misery.   True False

11.   I'll give up my addiction-of-choice soon, but not right now.   True False

*Step #6 Reflections:

I am entirely ready to examine my destructive **character defects**:

	Examples:	*Consequences:*
*Faults:	*	*
	*	*
*Failures:	*	*
	*	*
*Fascinations: *(obsessed with)*	*	*
	*	*
*Fabrications: (lies):	*	*
	*	*

*Application: Give Careful Consideration to:

Moses	**Five-Part-Plan**
God had a **plan** for <u>Moses</u>.	**Plan:** lead people through wilderness to the promised land
Moses **protested**. I have these character defects:	**Protest:** *I can't do it! *People won't believe me. *I'm not very good with words.
God **prepared** <u>Moses</u>:	**Preparation:** *40 years in the palace *40 years in the dessert
<u>Moses</u> **participated**. God's will **prevailed.**	**Participation:** Led Israelites through wilderness **Prevailed:** People arrived in promise land

Put **your name** in the blanks: Fill in this **Five-Part-Plan**:

God has a **plan** for _____ .

Plan: _____

_____

_____ **protests**.
I have these character defects:

Protest: * _____
* _____
* _____

God **prepares** _____ .

Preparation: * _____
* _____

_____ **participates**.

Participation: * _____
* _____

God's will **prevails**.

Prevails: * _____
* _____

*Greats!	Moses!	Me!
Great Kid!	Baby in Boat-Basket	*
Great Guy! *(Gal)*	Prince in Palace-40 Years	*
Great Goof!	Killed an Egyptian	*
Great Grief!	Fled to Desert-40 Years	*
Great God!	Attention Intervention/Burning Bush	*
Great Grace!	Protection in Wilderness Wanderings	*
Great Gratitude!	Wisdom, Guidance, Mercy	*

*Who did you share Step #6 and Moses' story with? _____
Reactions? _____

*Please identify 3 character defects that must no longer be part of your life.
What strategies are you going to use to ensure these defects do not return?
Character defects: *Strategies to eliminate:*

*   *

*   *

*   *

Please complete the following check sheet during the week:

Name _____   _____ Class
Dates: _____   _____ Brought Bible/Pencil
Class/Church Attendance   _____ Brought Extra Credit
Date: Class/Church Name: _____ Brought Journal

_____   _____
_____   _____   Memory Practice Step # 6
_____   _____   _____ Step # 6
_____   _____   _____ Memory Verse
_____   _____   _____ Extra Cr. Memory Verse

Devotions begin on p. 33   Bible Reading   Homework for Step # **6**
_____ Devotional #1   _____ Day #1   _____ Day #1
_____ Devotional #2   _____ Day #2   _____ Day #2
_____ Devotional #3   _____ Day #3   _____ Day #3
_____ Devotional #4   _____ Day #4   _____ Day #4
_____ Devotional #5   _____ Day #5   _____ Day #5
_____ Devotional #6   _____ Day #6   _____ Day #6
_____ Devotional #7   _____ Day #7   _____ Day #7

Please write your prayer requests below:

STTA: Good-Bye Letters to My Drug-of-Choice

From:	*Clean & Sober*	*Strongville,*	*God's Grace*
To:	*Budwieser*	*Loser Street*	*Drunkenville, Nowhere*

Dear Budweiser,
I know we have been friends for going on 9 years. When I had the courage to walk out of an abusive relationship, our celebration began. You were there to help me through the nights I spent alone when the boys went to their father's for the weekends. You were there to influence my decision of letting the boys live with their father. By my side you stayed when their father denied me my visitation rights. Throughout this time you never left me, not once. On those hot summer days as I worked up a sweat, there you were in my cooler buried under mountains of ice - ready to quench my thirst, to let me know my work day was complete. I must say goody-bye friend. I am older & wiser. My boys, now, are young men. I have found a friend in Jesus who intoxicates me with shots of grace and cases of love & faith. Sorry to let you down, but keep your head up; it's 5 o'clock somewhere.
Adios,   A. B.

From:	*New Life Coming*	*Peaceville, TN.*	
To:	*Pain Pills & All Pills*	*Lonelyville St. Brokenheartsville, TN 0000 Nowhere*	

Dear All Pills in My Old Life,
    We had a pretty good relationship I used to think. I always thought you were there for me every time I was hurting or needing to forget things! Yet here I sit again….all alone and hurting just as bad, if not worse, and I have pretty much lost everything because of you. I've lost my children's trust, my family's trust, and everything else in between!
    I have said many times that I was done with you and somehow always resorted right back to you. But this time I've asked the Lord to give me strength and courage to keep you away. I'm praying every morning and every night for that strength and courage. I refuse to let you rule my life anymore. I'm taking back over thanks to the Lord's help, and WE WILL DO IT! I will be seeing you no more. I'm starting a new life without you and going to live happily without you! (ME & GOD WITHOUT YOU!)
    GOOD-BYE FOREVER!   *M. H.*

From:	*32 Miserable Lane*	*Scared-to-Death, TN 38555*	*November 13, 2012*
To:	*Meth & Weed*	*124 Ruined-My-Life Ave, but I'm Gonna Be, OK, Thank God!*	

Dear Meth,
    I'm writing you this letter to tell you that I'm finally through. I've spent the last 13 years giving you my all and everything, and yes always graciously accepted you. I've loved you for so long that I have turned my back on my family, my husband, my own life, even my very own kids.
    I have taken so much for granted since I met you. You have absolutely been no good for me, giving me nothing in return for my loyalty. So now with that said, I'm done, finally done. I will no more be coming to you for comfort and understanding. You will no longer be my friend or my Savior.
    I have more - a new life with God, my real Savior, and my one and only true best friend. So good-bye meth. I never, never want to see you again!
Never Again Yours,   K. A.

Rejoice in Recovery 12-Step Faith-Based Study
Participant's Lesson
Step #7   Date _____
"For I know the plans I have for you," says the Lord.
"They are plans for good and not for disaster, to give you a future and a hope."
Jeremiah 29: 11

*Step #7 Smart Start
*Step #7:   Retrain Brain!   *Devotionals start on p. 915 LR Bible*
          We _____ asked God to _____ our _____.
*Step #7 Paraphrase: *Asked God to help me change.*
          If I could have changed myself, I would have done it a long time ago.
*Step #7 Key Terms: *change, habits, patterns of behavior, shortcomings*

*Step #7 Chant: *Choose to change! Choose to change!*
                              No more bondage for my brain!
                              Changed my brain! Changed my heart!
                              Now I'm getting habit-smart!!
*Review *(please use step wording)*:
Step #1: Admitted that _____
Step #2: Believe that _____
Step #3: Made a decision to _____
Step #4: Took a _____
Step #5: Admitted my wrongs to _____
Step #6: Was entirely ready to _____

*Step #7 Introduction: Transformation Implementation: Get Ready! Get Set! GO!
Are you in bondage to your shortcomings, *destructive attitudes and actions*?   Share:
1.   Examples of *alcohol/drug-related shortcomings* in your life?
          *
          *

2.   Examples of *sexually-related shortcomings* in your life?
          *
          *

3.   Examples of *money-related shortcomings* in your life including illegal means to
          obtain and/or illegal or unwise uses of money.
          *
          *

4.   What have you done on your own to try to remove these shortcomings,
          destructive attitudes and actions/bad habits, from your life?
          *
          *
          *

5.   Why haven't **you** been successful in removing **your** shortcomings?

6.   What have your **family** and **friends** done to try to help you remove shortcomings from your life?
     *
     *
     *

7.   How successful has their help been?

8.   What has **God** done to try to help you remove shortcomings from your life?
     *
     *
     *

9.   Why hasn't **God** been successful in removing your shortcomings?

You are **ready**, **willing**, and **able** to change when you:
     *Admit you have a problem
     *Accept full responsibility for your own faults and failures
     *Ask God humbly and sincerely for help in the removal of your destructive habits

Are you **ready** and **willing** to humbly **ask** God to remove your shortcomings? _____

10.   What are some advantages to God **instantly** removing your shortcomings?
     *
     *

11.   What are some reasons God might **not remove** your shortcomings **instantly** but assist in their removal over a period of time?
     *
     *

12.   A well-known quotation from George Santayana is, *"Those who do not learn from the past are condemned to repeat it."*
*What have you learned from your past? _____
*What will it cost you **to change**? _____
*What will it cost you **not to change**? _____
_____

Step #7 Memory Verse: *2 Corinthians 5: 17 (p. 1486)*
         Anyone who belongs to Christ   *Draw the old you &*
         *has become a **new person.***   *the new you:*
         *The **old life** is **gone**;*
         *a **new life** has **begun**!*

1.   Describe the new life you want: _____
         _____

2.   I have practiced writing this verse on the margins of this page and other pages in the homework _____ times and know this verse from memory. _____
                                                                       Signature

*Step #7 Extra Credit Verse: *Philippians 3: 13b-14 (p. 1525)*
> *Forgetting the **past** and looking **forward** to what lies ahead,*   Draw you
> *I **press** on to reach the end of the **race***   winning the
> *and receive the heavenly **prize***   race:
> *for which God, through Christ Jesus, is **calling** us.*

1. What do you get if you run the race with Jesus? _____
   _____

2. I have practiced writing this verse on the margins of this page and other pages in the homework _____ times and know this verse from memory. _____
                     Signature

*Step #7 Bible Stories: Choose-to-Change Trilogy
    *The Demon Possessed Man   Insanity-Related Behaviors
    *A Woman Caught in Adultery   Sexually-Related Shortcomings
    *Samson & Delilah   Sexual/Money-Related Shortcomings

*Jesus Heals a Demon-Possessed Man: Insanity-Related Behaviors
Luke 8: 26-39 (pp. 1303-1304)

Demon-Possessed Man	**Me**
1. Evidence of **insanity**?	**Evidence of **insanity** in my life?
*	*
*	*
*	*
*	*
2. Sanity returns. **Change** in man's appearance & emotions?	**Sanity returns. **Change** in my appearance & emotions?
*	*
*	*
3. Town people's **reaction** to change?	**Frenemies **reaction** to change?
*	*
*	*
4. What did Jesus tell the man **to do**?	**What does Jesus tell me **to do**?
*	*
*	*
5. What did the man **do**?	**What are you going **to do**?
*	*

6. What are some demons, *addictions*, that hold you in bondage?
    *   *
    *   *

7. If you make a **decision** to turn your **will** and your **life** over to the care of God and allow Him to set you free from any *addiction-bondage,* what **changes** will occur in your life?
    *   *

    *   *

*A Woman Caught in Adultery: Sexually-Related Shortcomings
John 8: 1-11 (pp. 1353-1354)

Woman	**Me**
1. What happened when she **got caught** doing something illegal? *	**What could happen when you get **caught** doing something illegal? *
2. What was her **lawful penalty**? *	**What is your **lawful penalty**? *
3. What do you think Jesus **wrote** in the **dust**? *	**What does Jesus **write** on your **heart**? *
4. How did Jesus **help** her? * *	**How does Jesus **help** you? * *
5. What **changes** did Jesus tell her to make? *	**What **changes** does Jesus tell you to make? * *

Note: "The evidence of forgiveness is a changed life." (Serendipity Bible, p. 1490)

*Samson & Delilah: Sexual/Money-Related Shortcomings
Judges 13-16 (pp. 320+)

Samson or Delilah	**Me**
1. Evidence **S** obsessed with **sex**: * * *	**Evidence you're obsessed with **sex**: * * *
2. Evidence **S** could be **manipulated**: * * *	**Evidence you can be **manipulated**: * * *
3. Evidence **S** was consumed with desire for **revenge**: * * *	**Evidence you're consumed with desire for **revenge**: * * *

4. Evidence **S** was an accomplished **liar**:
*
*
*

Evidence you're an accomplished **liar:
*
*
*

5. **Changes S** should have made,
but he **didn't**:
*
*
*

****Changes** you should make,
but you **haven't**:
*
*
*

6. Evidence **D** was **obsessed** with getting **money**:
*

Evidence you're **obsessed with getting **money**:
*

*

7. Evidence **D** was **manipulative**:
*
*
*

Evidence you're **manipulative:
*
*
*

8. Evidence **S** repented:
*

Evidence you're **repenting:
*

9. Evidence **God forgave S**:
*

Evidence **God forgives you:
*

*Step #7: Did You Get It? *(NA; 12/12; and Beattie Insight)
*Please circle True or False, and **explain why** you made each choice:

1. To get the right help in removing shortcomings from my life,   True False
    it is essential that I ask the right person for help.

2. When I want a shortcoming removed from my life, if I work   True False
    hard enough, I can get rid of any character defect on my own.

3. Shortcomings in my life cause pain, misery, insanity,   True False
    and destruction.

4. In some areas, my progress in recovery will be slow   True False

5. God will straighten my life out, if I'm willing to **wait** for
    His help.   True False

6.   I am sick and tired of being sick and tired.   True False

7.   Prayer is essential in the removal of my shortcomings.   True False

8.   The focus of my daily life should be love for God, others,   True False
        and myself.

9.   A basic ingredient of humility is seeking to do God's will.   True False

10.   I want freedom from the shackles of my addictions and am   True   False
        willing to do whatever it takes to be free.

11.   God often works through family, friends in my church, and
        AA, NA, and 12-Step Faith-Based meetings to make me aware
        of my shortcomings.   True   False

*AA Prayer *(based on the prayer in the AA Big Book, p. 76)*
Make a choice from each pair of words, and write your choice in the blank:

My Creator,
I am _____willing that _____ should have all of me, the
    (now, not)   (my drug-of-choice, you)
good and _____ the bad.
       (most of, all of)
I pray that you will _____ remove from me _____ defect/s of
         (in the future, now)   (some, every)
character which stand/s in the way of my usefulness to _____ and my
                               (me; you)
_____. Grant me _____ to do _____ bidding.
(frenemies, friends)   (weakness, strength)   (my; your)
Amen.

*Application:

**Pride says,   *I can do it myself.*
**Humility says,   *I can't do it myself. Please help me.*
      Note: Humility includes teach-ability.

1.   Share a situation in your life when you had trouble asking for help.

2.   Share a situation in your life when you asked God and another human being for
        help.

3.   What are your fears about becoming changed?

*

*

*

4.   What would you like to see changed about you?

     *

     *

     *

5.   How can you go about making these changes?

     *

     *

     *

6.   Share ways you are focusing more on God and less on yourself.

     *

     *

     *

*Meditate on this **humility** acrostic.
Write a personal prayer asking for help.

H-Honestly   Dear God,
U-Understanding   Thank you for changing me.
M-Myself as   Thank you for _____
I-I am.   _____
L-Letting go of   _____
I-Illusions that, "I'm right."   Please help me _____
T-Totally Transformed into   _____
Y-Your Image   _____
                                      _____
                                      _____
                                      _____

* Step #7 Reflections:
*My Transformation Celebration
Hint: Check out Galatians 5: 16-26 (p. 1505); Proverbs 16 (p. 804)

My super-seven **new smart habits**:   Strategies for developing these habits:

*   *

*   *

*   *

*   *

*   *

*   *

*   *

*Who did you share Step #7 and The Choose-to-Change Trilogy with? _____
Reactions? _____

Please complete the following check sheet during the week:

Name _____
Dates: _____
Class/Church Attendance
Date: Class/Church Name:

_____   _____
_____   _____
_____   _____
_____   _____
_____   _____

_____ Class
_____ Brought Bible/Pencil
_____ Brought Extra Credit
_____ Brought Journal

Memory Practice Step #7
_____ Step #7
_____ Memory Verse
_____ Extra Cr. Memory Verse

Devotions begin on p. 915	Bible Reading	Homework for Step #7
_____ Devotional #1	_____ Day #1	_____ Day #1
_____ Devotional #2	_____ Day #2	_____ Day #2
_____ Devotional #3	_____ Day #3	_____ Day #3
_____ Devotional #4	_____ Day #4	_____ Day #4
_____ Devotional #5	_____ Day #5	_____ Day #5
_____ Devotional #6	_____ Day #6	_____ Day #6
_____ Devotional #7	_____ Day #7	_____ Day #7

Please write your prayer requests below:

STTA: **Good-bye Letter to My Drug-of-Choice**

A New Me
777 Fresh Start Ln.
Crossville, TN 38555
November 13, 2012

My Biggest Weakness
66 Skummy Ln
Crossville, TN 38555

Dear My Biggest Weakness, "Meth,"

Well, let me start by saying, you used to make me feel strong. But as you pulled me down into the depths of your hell, I was blind to what you really were! I trusted you. You were always there whether I felt sad, lonely, depressed, or just wanted to have fun and smile! But now I see you were just using me! The more I gave, the more you took. And before I even knew it, you took everything from me: my marriage, my children, my ambition, houses, cars, my friends, everything that made me secure. And you replaced all of that with: unfaithfulness, loneliness, homelessness, brokenness, and insecurities! Even then you were not done.

As if you had not taken enough from me, you were relentless. You took my hope and my love for myself, and you turned my career of nursing and raising my children into dealing drugs. You made me weaker than anyone I know. Now don't get me wrong, I played a part too. You already see I turned to you, and trusted you too. I gave you my freedom!!
            Just look what you have done!
            You are even more deadly than a damn gun!
You have killed me from the inside out. But today is the day I'm saying, GOOD-BYE! And taking my life BACK! It may take time. And I know it won't be easy! But, with God's help, I will find myself! I will earn the trust of my mother and my children again. I will pick up the pieces of my life and start putting them back together again. I know you will be there following me around, trying to slip back into my life. But I promise, you will never again be as strong as you were before. Because I now know that my family and God's love and forgiveness, along with the memories that you've taught me- they will build a wall, and you will NEVER get back in.

So I'm taking back all the trust I gave you and placing it in God's hands. You can NEVER have it back again. I'm DONE!!! So GOOD-BYE FOREVER! I'm no longer your slave. God has replaced the Devil that you put in my heart, body, and mind to blind me. I NO LONGER choose meth over my family, my children, and ME!

GOOD-BYE to My biggest weakness, "Meth." I have traded you for STRENGTH, my family, my children, myself, and God"
No regrets, only Lessons, S. J.
       P.S. I now know you were the weak one, not me!
       Note: Envelope-Sealed with love & honesty

Rejoice in Recovery 12-Step Faith-Based Study
Participant's Lesson
Step #<u>8</u>   Date _____
"For I know the plans I have for you," says the Lord.
"They are plans for good and not for disaster, to give you a future and a hope." Jeremiah 29: 11

*Smart Step Start
*Step #8:   Fence-Mending List #1   *LRB Devotionals Start on Page 107*
We made a _____ of all persons we had _____ and
became _____ to make _____ to them all.
*Step #8 Paraphrase: *Write down the names of those I hurt.*
*Step #8 Key Terms: *acknowledge, amend, harm*
*Step #8 Chant: *Who'd I harm? Make a list. On forgiveness, God insists!*

*Review *(please use step wording):*
Step #6: My preparation for transformation involves getting **entirely ready (ER)** and
willing for God to _____
Step #7: My transformation implementation begins when I humbly _____
_____

*Step #8 Introduction: The Fear of Forgiveness
1.   What are some ways I may have **harmed** someone *(I-O-U)*? *(Harm means to intentionally or unintentionally cause physical or mental damage through words, actions, or lack of action.)*
        *   *
        *   *

2.   An **apology** and an **amend** for harming someone are **not** the same thing. Often when I apologize by saying, **"I'm sorry,"** I accept no responsibility for the harm I've done. Saying, "I'm sorry," could mean:
                                Personal examples from your life:
        *I'm **sorry** you caught me: _____
        _____
        *I'm **sorry,** but it wasn't my fault: _____
        _____
        *I'm **sorry** I'm getting in trouble: _____
        _____
        *I'm **sorry** you don't see this my way: _____
        _____

3.   How do I often react to people **I have harmed/hurt** *(I-O-U)*?
                        Specific examples of a time I did this:
        *Avoid: _____
        _____
        *Attack *(in your face confrontation)*:_____
        _____
        *Gossip about: _____
        _____

4.   **Favorite Rationalizations NOT to Forgive** *(Thanks, Janis Keeling)*

My Super-Duper-I'll-Not-Forgive-You Excuses: Examples from your life:

*The offense was too great: _____

*She won't accept responsibility: _____

*He isn't truly sorry: _____

*She has never asked to be forgiven: _____

*He'll do it again: _____

*I don't like her: _____

*He did it deliberately: _____

*If I forgive, I'll have to be nice to her: _____

*Someone has to punish him: _____

*I can't forgive, because I'll never forget: _____

*I'd be a hypocrite to say I'll forgive her, because I don't want to forgive her: _____

_____

5.   What does God say I should do when **I have harmed/hurt** someone *(I-O-U)?*
        (Hint: Matthew 5: 23-24 p. 1203) _____

        _____

6.   How do I often react to people **who have harmed/hurt me** *(U-O-Me)?*
                                        Specific examples of a time I did this:
        *Avoid: _____

        _____

        *Attack *(in-your-face confrontation)*: _____

        _____

        *Gossip about: _____

        _____

7.   What is a **consequence** for me if I **choose** <u>not</u> to forgive others *(U-O-Me)?* Hint:
        see Matthew 6: 14-15 (p. 1205) This is an explanation for Matthew 6: 12 in "The Lord's Prayer."

        _____

8.   To for**GIVE** means to **give up** resentment and the desire to-get-even. Share a
        situation when you **forgave** someone even though he/she had done some terrible,
        horrible, no good, very bad things to you.   _____

        _____

*Step #8 Memory Verses: *Colossians 3: 13 (p. 1534)*
                *Make **<u>allowance</u>** for each other's **<u>faults</u>**, and*
                *forgive anyone who **<u>offends</u>** you. (U-O-Me)*
                *Remember, the Lord forgave **<u>you</u>**,*
                *so you **<u>must</u>** forgive others.*

1.   What does God say I **must do** for someone who has **harmed/offended me**
        (U-O-Me)? _____

        _____

2.   I have practiced writing this verse on the margins of this page and other pages in
        the homework _____ times and know this verse from memory . _____
                                                                Signature

*Extra Credit Verse: *Matthew 11: 28   (LRB p. 1214)*
*Come unto **me**, all of you who are **weary** and carry heavy **burdens**,
and I will give you **rest.***

1.   If I **choose** to ask God for help with my burden of making amends to those I have
harmed *(I-O-U)*, how will God help me? _____

_____

2.   I have practiced writing this verse on the margins of this page and other pages in
the homework _____ times and know this verse from memory. _____
                                                                              Signature

*Step #7 Bible Story: **Joseph the Forgiver**

*Joseph's Dreams *Genesis 37: 1-17 (pp. 54-55)*

1.   Explain why Joseph's brothers hated him in each of the following areas:
*Father's favorite: _____
*Tattletale Teenager: _____
*Robe: _____
*Dream #1: _____
*Family reaction to dream: _____

_____
*Dream #2: _____
*Family reaction to dream: _____

_____

*Joseph Sold into Slavery *Genesis 37: 18-36 (pp. 55-56)*
Note: Cistern: deep hole in ground for holding water

1.   **Plan #1**: How did the brothers first plan to get rid of Joseph?
_____

2.   **Plan #2**: Reuben intervened, and offered them an alternative.
*What did Reuben suggest? _____
*What was the advantage of this plan? _____
*What did the brothers do right after throwing him into the cistern that indicated
they weren't concerned about Joseph's impending death? _____

3.   **Plan #3**: Ishmaelite/Midianite traders came by.
*What was Plan #3? _____
*What were the advantages of this plan? _____

_____

4.   The brothers were insensitive to their father's feelings and took Joseph's blood-
covered robe to him. Jacob assumed his son was dead. Share an example from
your past about when you did something wrong, and you weren't concerned about
others' feelings?

5.   What did the Ishmaelite/Midianite traders do with Joseph?

*Joseph in Potiphar's House   *Genesis 39: 1-16 (pp. 58-59)*

1.   Explain the predicament in which Joseph found himself?

2.   How did Joseph try to deal with this difficult situation?

3.   Why would sleeping with Potiphar's wife be a sin against God?

4.   Why did Potiphar's wife lie?
        *
        *
        *

5.   Give an example of when someone lied about **you** to keep from getting himself/herself in trouble.

6.   Potiphar's wife found herself in a *"temptation situation."* When you find yourself temped by a sexy guy or gorgeous gal, how **should you** deal with the situation?

*Joseph Put in Prison   *Genesis 39: 19-23 (pp. 59-60)*

1.   During his long-term in prison, Joseph didn't *sit-and-sulk* while moaning aloud, "It's not my fault! I didn't do anything wrong!" What did he do instead? *(Hint: Serenity prayer devotional for what to do when life treats us unfairly (p. 55)*

2.   Give an example of a time when something happened to you that wasn't fair, but then God turned it around for good.

*Joseph Interprets Two Dreams   *Genesis 40 (p. 60)*

1.   Whose job is dream interpretation? _____
2.   What kinds of problems might we have if we try to interpret our own dreams?

3.   What kinds of problems might we have if we ask our *frenemies* to interpret our dreams?

*Pharaoh's Dreams *Genesis 41 (pp. 60-62)*

1.   The cup-bearer forgot about Joseph for two years. How would you react if you had to spend 2 additional years in jail/prison when you didn't deserve to be there?

2.   How did Joseph know what Pharaoh's dreams meant? *(Hint: see 41: 16)*

3.   When Joseph got out of prison, what was his new job description, and what was he given?
      *
      *

*Joseph's Brothers Go to Egypt *Genesis 42 (pp. 63-64)*
Note: Brothers last saw him when he was @17 years old. He is now @40 years old.

1.   What did Joseph do when he recognized his brothers?
      *
      *

2.   Why didn't Joseph identify himself when his brothers first met with him?

3.   Why did Joseph put his brothers in prison? *(Hint: footnote 42: 22)*

4.   Why did Joseph's brothers think they were put in prison?

*Joseph Reveals His Identity *Genesis 45 (pp. 67-68; Hint: look at footnotes)*

1.   What do you suppose the brothers' fears were when they found out Joseph was alive and second in command in Egypt?
      *
      *

2.   How did Joseph comfort his brothers?
      *
      *
      *

3.   If your family hated you, lied about you, abused you, and/or sold you, how could you ever forgive them?
      *

      *

*Step #8 Did You Get It?
Please circle True or False, and **explain why** you made each choice.

I am NOT going to make amends because: *(Thanks Tom Hall)*

1. Some offenses are so small that no amend is necessary.   True False

2. We are getting along so well now, the past is best forgotten.   True False

3. Making the amends will involve money that I don't have,
   so I can't make amends.   True False

4. This is not a good time for me. I'll do it later.   True False

5. The other person was mostly wrong.   True False

6. If I honestly try to never do it again, no amend is necessary.   True False

Think about the following statements regarding forgiveness.   *(Thanks Janis Keeling)*

1. I have to maintain a friendship with each person I've forgiven.   True False

2. When I forgive, I must forget.   True False

3. I have to forgive those who hurt, abused, molested, deceived,
   or lied to me.   True False

4. When I forgive, I give up the right to get even.   True False

5. When I agree to forgive someone who has harmed me, this
   means that what he/she did was OK.   True False

R. T. Kendall (2007) says we must forgive ourselves totally.
1. Satan wants me to forgive myself.   True False

2. Forgiving myself will give me inner peace and freedom
   from the bondage of guilt.   True False

3. When I don't forgive myself, I suffer
   mentally, **e**motionally, **s**ocially and **s**piritually.   True False

*4-A + 1 Amend: *Something to Think About*
- ***A**dmit my guilt   *I was wrong*
- ***A**cknowledge type of offense   *When I <u>lied to you</u>*
- ***A**ssure best effort not do again   *I'll do my best not to <u>lie to you again</u>.*
- ***A**sk for forgiveness   *Will you please forgive me?*
- ***A**ttempt to repair damage   *(will depend on situation)*

*Make entries on the following charts:

*Joseph's U-O-Me Amends List
List of people who harmed Joseph, people he needed to forgive

Who harmed Joseph?	What did they do to Joseph?
*Brothers	*
*Potiphar's Wife	*
*Potiphar	*
*Pharaoh's Cup-bearer	*

*My U-O-Me Amends List
List of people who have harmed me, people I need to forgive

Who harmed me?	What did they do to me?
*	*
*	*
*	*

*My I-O-U Amends List
List of people I have harmed, people I want to forgive me

Who have I harmed?	What did I do to them?
*	*
*	*
*	*

*My I-O-Me Amends List
List of things I have done to myself, things I need to forgive myself for

What have I done to myself?	Why do I have to forgive myself?
*	*
*	*
*	*

*My I-O-God Amends List
List of shortcomings that I want God to forgive me for

What do I want God to forgive me for?	How do I know God will forgive me?
*	*
*	*
*	*

*Step #8: Reflections:
1.   **12 Stupid Things that Mess Up Recovery** *by Allen Berger*
            Stupid Thing 6: Not Making Amends
         "To develop a strong spiritual foundation for recovery
         it is essential that we accept full responsibility for
         our harmful and hurtful behavior and that we attempt
         to repair the damage that we have caused
         in our relationships with our family, friends, and loved ones." *(p. 51)*
Of course you do not want fall into the trap of *Stupid Thing 6.*
Please identify four changes you are going to make in your life **regarding forgiveness,**
so that you will not mess up your recovery:
      *   *
      *   *

2.   The Bible teaches us to live in   *My Prayer for Harmony:*
      Harmony as we: Dear God,
      H-Humbly make   ·   Please help me live in harmony with
      A-Amends and work toward   _____
      R-Reconciliation because of God's   _____
      M-Mercy and His unfailing love.   _____
      O-Overcoming   Please guide me in making amends
      N-Negativity   to _____
      Y-Yesterday, today, and forever   _____
                                       _____
                                       _____

3.   Who did you Share Step #8 and Joseph's story with? _____
      Reactions? _____

Please complete the following check sheet during the week:

Name _____   _____ Class
Dates: _____   _____ Brought Bible/Pencil
Class/Church Attendance   _____ Brought Extra Credit
Date: Class/Church Name: _____ Brought Journal

_____   _____   Memory Practice Step #8
_____   _____   _____ Step # 8
_____   _____   _____ Memory Verse
_____   _____   _____ Extra Cr. Memory Verse

Devotions begin on p. 107   Bible Reading   Homework for Step #8
_____ Devotional #1   _____ Day #1   _____ Day #1
_____ Devotional #2   _____ Day #2   _____ Day #2
_____ Devotional #3   _____ Day #3   _____ Day #3
_____ Devotional #4   _____ Day #4   _____ Day #4
_____ Devotional #5   _____ Day #5   _____ Day #5
_____ Devotional #6   _____ Day #6   _____ Day #6
_____ Devotional #7   _____ Day #7   _____ Day #7

Please write your prayer requests below:

STTA: **Poems to Ponder**

Don't Give Up on Me

These brick walls and metal doors they hold me in,
Cause I was living a life full of sin.

The pill, the needle the feel of the poke.
Some people think that it's all a joke.

The high that I feel when the blood comes in.
I know that it's killing me, but I do it again.

This addiction that I fight is tearing me apart.
It has taken me away from the ones in my heart.

So I pray to the Lord every day and night.
I have started this battle. Please help me win this fight.

Cause I can't go on, on my own anymore,
And I feel like I'm knocking on death's door.

So to all the ones that I love and who care,
I am slowly but surely getting there.

So don't give up on me without a fight.
Pray for me with all of your might.
Cause we've got God on our side tonight!   *B. W.*

Thank You God

Thank you for finding me when I was lost.
Taking that shortcut sure took a cost.
Many times you've come for me when I needed a hand.
Little did I know, you are always right behind me, there you stand.

I love you, and I am so thankful I've received this 2nd chance.
In your name I will rejoice and dance.
Although I know this regret I feel,
Will slowly fade with you and not a pill or a drug deal.

With you I've gained the strength to fight back.
You make up where I lack.
For that I've always known,
My vision and focus were just blurred with the Devil's tone.
Thank you God for letting me return home!   *S. M.*

Rejoice in Recovery 12-Step Faith-Based Study
Participant's Lesson
Step #9   **Date** _____
"For I know the plans I have for you," says the Lord.
"They are plans for good and not for disaster, to give you a future and a hope."
Jeremiah 29: 11

*Smart Step Start   *LRB Devotionals Start on Page 49*
*Step #9:   Fence-Mending Action
We made _____ _____ to such people whenever _____, except when to do
so would _____ them or _____. *(ask for forgiveness)*
*Step #9 Paraphrase: *Fix what I can without hurting anyone else.*
*Step #9 Key Terms: *acknowledge, amend, harm*
*Steps #9 Chant: **I'll forgive. I'll forgive.*   *I'll forgive, cause I want to live!*
                             *Forgive you. (U-O-Me)   *You forgive me. (I-O-U)*
                             Forgive myself; (I-O-Me)   *Then let it be!*

*Review Step #8:

My I-O-U amends list for   My U-O-Me amends list for
people **I harmed** includes the   people **who harmed me** includes the
following names: following names:
*   *   *   *
*   *   *   *

*Step #9 Introduction: **The Freedom of Forgiveness: Practice Makes Perfect**
                                (Based on AA; NA; 12/12; Beattie; and Hall)
1. When making a direct **4-A + 1 Amend**:   **4-A + 1 Amend Example:**
        *Admit my guilt   **I was wrong*
        *Acknowledge type of offense   **When I lied to you*
        *Assure best effort not do again   **I'll do my best not to lie to you again.*
        *Ask for forgiveness   **Will you please forgive me?*
        *Attempt to repair damage   **(will depend on situation)*

2.   Personal **4-A+ 1** Amend example #1:   Personal **4-A + 1** Amend example #2:
        *I was wrong   **I was wrong*
        *When I _____   **When I* _____
        *I'll do my best not to   **I'll do my best not to*

        _____   _____
        *Will you please forgive me?   **Will you please forgive me?*
        *Please allow me to _____   **Please allow me to* _____

3.   Share a personal example in which you decided **not** to ask the
        person you harmed *(I-O-U)* for forgiveness.
        Example: *Impact on you:*   *Impact on the other person:*

4.   Joyce Myers says **not** forgiving the **person who harmed you** *(U-O-Me)*
        is like taking poison and hoping the person, you won't forgive, will die. Share a
        personal example when you choose **not** to forgive someone who **harmed you** and
        what **impact** this **un-forgiveness** has had on your life.

How Do We Ask for Forgiveness?
*Direct Amend Strategies: (1) face-to-face (2) telephone call, and (3) letter or email

	Advantages:	*Disadvantages:*
1.	Face-to-Face: * *	Face-to-Face: * *
2.	Telephone Call: * *	Telephone Call: * *
3.	Letter or Email: * *	Letter or Email: * *

4.   Share an example of a **face-to-face** amend you are going to make: _____
_____

Explain why a **face-to-face** amend is best in this situation: _____
_____

5.   Share an example of a **telephone call** amend you are going to make: _____
_____

Explain why a **telephone call** amend is best in this situation: _____
_____

6.   Share an example of **letter or email** amend you are going to make: _____
_____

Explain why a **letter or email** amend is best in this situation: _____
_____

***Indirect Amend Decisions**
Who? An **indirect amend is recommended when the person **you harmed** and to whom you should make the amend:

    *Would be hurt/harmed   *Can't be located

    *Doesn't realize hurt/harm has occurred   *Has passed away

How? Possibilities for making an **indirect amend include:

    ***Letter**-to be shared **only** with a counselor, sponsor, or trusted friend;
        may be destroyed

    ***Community Service**-homeless shelter, soup kitchen, nursing home, etc.

    ***Personal Recovery Story**-sharing to help others

1.   Share an example in which you will **not** make a direct amend for fear of **hurting/harming** the person: _____

How will you make this **indirect amend**? _____

2.   Share an example where you **can't locate** the person to whom you should make the amend: _____
How will you make this **indirect amend**: _____
_____

3.   Share an example in which the person does **not realize** you have harmed him/her (e.g., children): _____

_____

How will you make this **indirect amend**: _____

_____

4.   Share a situation in which the person to whom you should make the amend has passed away: _____
How will you make this **indirect amend**: _____

_____

*Restitution Decisions
Restitution includes: *Restoring something that has been wrongfully taken away*
                         Compensating for loss, damage, or injury

5.   Share a personal situation for which you need to make **financial restitution: ____**

_____

How will you make arrangements for payment: _____

_____

*Amends: Now, Later, or Never
1.   If I choose to make amends **now**, what are the consequences?
      *
      *

2.   If I choose to make amends **later**, what are the consequences?
      *
      *

3.   If I choose to make amends **never**, what are the consequences?
      *
      *

4.   What are some of the **excuses** I use for **not** making amends?
      *
      *

*Step #9 Memory Verse: *Matthew 18: 21-22 (p. 1226) Peter asked,*
      "Lord, how often should I forgive someone who sins against me? Seven times?"
      "No!" Jesus replied. "Seventy times seven!"

1.   Who is the person you have forgiven the most times, and why do you continue to forgive this person?_____

2.   I have practiced writing this verse on the margins of this page and other pages in the homework _____ times and know this verse from memory. _____
                                                                              Signature

*Step #9 Extra Credit Verse: *(Luke 6: 27-28, p. 1299)*
But to you who are willing to listen, I (Jesus) say,

*Love your **enemies**!*
*Do good to those who **hate** you.*
*Bless those who **curse** you.*
*Pray for those who **hurt** you.*

*What changes will you have to make in your life if
you follow these verses? _____
_____
_____
_____
_____

2.   I have practiced writing this verse on the margins of this page and other pages in
        the homework _____ times and know this verse from memory. _____
                                                                              Signature

*Step #9 Bible Story: Simon Peter: From Fisherman to Fisher-of-Men
Fill-in-the-Blanks. Find answers in Peter's Biography and side column on p. 1251
Simon Peter's job: _____   *Note: He will become a fisher-of-men.*
Jesus gave Simon a nickname _____ that means _____
Peter was a recognized _____ and _____ for the 12 _____
The two books in the New Testament that Peter wrote are _____ and _____

*Peter's Faith: Get-Out-of-the-Boat, Walk-on-Water Faith *Matthew 14: 22-33 (p. 1220)*
1.   How was Jesus being *recharged* when the disciples got into trouble? _____
        What was He modeling for us? *(Hint: see LRB footnote 14: 22-23)* _____
        _____

2.   Disciples' reactions when they saw Jesus walking on the water? _____
        What did they think they saw? _____

3.   How did Peter demonstrate his **faith?** _____

4.   How did Peter demonstrate his **fear**? _____

5.   What was Peter's prayer, perhaps the shortest prayer in the Bible? _____

6.   How can you demonstrate your willingness to *get-out-of-the-boat* (the comfort of
        your addiction) and *walk-on-the-water* with Jesus?
        (Challenge: illustrate your answer)

7.   How can you overcome a *take-your-eyes-off-Jesus, sure-to-sink* way of thinking?

*Peter's Faults: Get Me a Calculator   *Matthew 18: 21-35 (p. 1226-1227)*
1.   Peter suggested to Jesus that forgiving someone ____ times should be more than
        sufficient. Jesus replied that he should forgive _____ which is _____ times.
        How many times should you forgive someone? _____
2.   What is Jesus teaching us *The Parable of the Unforgiving Debtor?* _____
        _____

3.   Using information from 1 Corinthians 13: 5 *(p. 1471)*, what was Jesus teaching
        his disciples and you about forgiveness? _____

*Peter-Foreshadowing   *Luke 22: 31-34 (p. 1330)*
1.   How did Jesus provide support for Peter for the troubled times ahead?

2.   Jesus predicted that Peter will; _____
        Peter's response to Jesus' concern: _____

*Peter Forsakes Jesus: Rejection *Luke 22: 54-62 (p. 1331-32; FN p. 1330)*
1.   What did Peter say when questioned about being with Jesus?
        a. Denial #1 _____
        b. Denial #2 _____
        c. Denial #3 _____

2.   What happened that reminded Peter of Jesus' denial prediction:
        _____
        _____

3.   What was Peter's response when he realized that he had denied Jesus?
        _____

*Peter's Forgiven: Restoration & Responsibility *John 21: 15-17 (p. 1376; FN)*
1.   Jesus' questions to Peter were: *(Hint: slight differences)*
        a. Question #1 _____
        b. Question #2 _____
        c. Question #3 _____

2.   After each of Peter's responses, Jesus gave him a job to do: *(Hint: slight differences)*
        a. Job #1 _____
        b. Job #2 _____
        c. Job #3 _____

*My Rejection, Restoration, & Responsibility:
1.   I denied Jesus when I: _____
        Jesus would probably ask me: _____
        Jesus would probably give me the following job to do: _____
        _____

2.   I denied Jesus when I: _____
        Jesus would probably ask me: _____
        Jesus would probably give me the following job to do: _____
        _____

3.   I denied Jesus when I: _____
        Jesus would probably ask me: _____
        Jesus would probably give me the following job to do: _____
        _____

*Peter Preaches to a Crowd *(early church sermon)* *Acts 2: 14-41 (pp. 1382-1383)*
1.   When Peter's words pierced the hearts of those in the crowd, what kind of
        decision did 3,000 people make?
        *   *

        *   *

*Peter's Miraculous Escape from Prison *Acts 12: 1-19 (pp. 1399-1400)*
1.   How did Peter's prison break occur?

2.   What was the reaction of the people who had been praying for Peter?

*Step #9: Did You Get It? *(based on AA, NA, 12/12, Hall, Kendall)*
Please circle True or False, and **explain why** you made each choice:

1.	My responsibility is to ask for forgiveness whether or not the person **I harmed** forgives me *(I-O-U)*.	True False
2.	Making amends may require financial restitution.	True False
3.	When I forgive someone who **harmed me**, I am saying he/she has done nothing wrong *(U-O-Me)*.	True False
4.	Forgiveness means I approve of what the person did to me.	True False
5.	Not forgiving someone has no impact on relapse.	True False
6.	Making contributions to those in my community is one way to make indirect amends.	True False
7.	I have to forgive someone whether or not I feel like forgiving.	True False
8.	Forgiveness means I have to let the person back into my life.	True False
9.	God didn't wait until I became sinless to forgive me, therefore I shouldn't expect others to become sinless to deserve my forgiveness.	True False
10.	I must right the wrong I have done to someone else whether or not he/she did something wrong to me.	True False
11.	To forgive and remember is only possible because of God's grace.	True False

*Fill out the following I-O U-Amend Forms: *(explanation without elaboration)*

_____I owe you an amend for hurting you.
(person's name)
I was wrong when I _____
                              (offense)
I'll do my best not to _____. Will you please forgive me?
Please allow me to _____
                        (attempt to repair damage)

_____I owe you an amend for hurting you.
(person's name)
I was wrong when I _____
                              (offense)
I'll do my best not to _____ Will you please forgive me?
Please allow me to _____
                        (attempt to repair damage)

_____I owe you an amend for hurting you.
(person's name)
I was wrong when I _____
                              (offense)
I'll do my best not to _____ Will you please forgive me?
Please allow me to _____
                        (attempt to repair damage)

_____I owe you an amend for hurting you.
(person's name)
I was wrong when I _____
                              (offense)
I'll do my best not to _____ Will you please forgive me?
Please allow me to _____
                        (attempt to repair damage)

_____I owe you an amend for hurting you.
(person's name)
I was wrong when I _____
                              (offense)
I'll do my best not to _____ Will you please forgive me?
Please allow me to _____
                        (attempt to repair damage)

*Step #9 Reflections:
*The Epitome of Forgiveness:

1.   When Jesus was crucified, why did He ask God, His Father, to forgive those who crucified Him? *(Hint: see Luke 23: 34, p. 1333)* _____

_____

2.   When Stephen was stoned and died, for whom did he ask forgiveness?
(Hint: Acts 7: 57-60; p. 1391) _____

_____

3.   Why would Jesus and Stephen be phenomenal role models in your journey to experience *the freedom of forgiveness*? _____

_____

_____

*Who did you discuss Step #9 and Peter's story with? _____
Reactions? _____

*I am going to improve my ability to make amends using the following 3 strategies:
        *

        *

        *

Please complete the following check sheet during the week:

Name _____   _____ Class
Dates: _____   _____ Brought Bible/Pencil
Class/Church Attendance   _____ Brought Extra Credit
Date: Class/Church Name: _____ Brought Journal

_____   _____
_____   _____   Memory Practice Step #9
_____   _____   _____ Step #9
_____   _____   _____ Memory Verse
_____   _____   _____ Extra Cr. Memory Verse

Devotions begin on p. 49   Bible Reading   Homework for Step **9**
_____ Devotional #1   _____ Day #1   _____ Day #1
_____ Devotional #2   _____ Day #2   _____ Day #2
_____ Devotional #3   _____ Day #3   _____ Day #3
_____ Devotional #4   _____ Day #4   _____ Day #4
_____ Devotional #5   _____ Day #5   _____ Day #5
_____ Devotional #6   _____ Day #6   _____ Day #6
_____ Devotional #7   _____ Day #7   _____ Day #7

Please write your prayer requests below:

STTA: Fear, Failure, and Freedom - Maybe

Fear of Freedom

I've been locked away for many a year,
Now it's close to freedom, and I'm full of fear.
When I step in the world that's so brand new,
How will I cope? What will I do?
> I should be happy that I'm going home,
> But those feelings of dread won't leave me alone.
> I say to myself, "Am I in control,
> Or will dope, once again, possess my soul?"

Will I stay with Jesus when I'm free?
Or will Satan grab a hold of me?
I'm getting ready to walk out this prison door
With those thoughts in my head and many more.
> Life is a gamble; achievement a must.
> I've got to make it! In God I trust.
> I must believe in myself, so I will not fail.
> I will NOT come back to more time in jail.

When my old friends start hanging around,
And offer… will I turn them down?
Night after night I lay here and pray,
Asking the Lord to show me the way.
> Right now, I'm with Jesus, and I'm free of sin.
> But when I hit the world, will the devil step in?
> My freedom's real close, but I'm not in a hurry,
> How I can remember? The world in my head is so blurry.

Jesus stay with me. Please help me to cope.
Give me the courage, the faith, and the hope.
I think of my family, and my heart wants to bust.
Will I ever win back their love and their trust?
> What about my children when I get home?
> Will they forgive me for leaving them alone?
> Well, when I get home, whatever I find,
> I'll just have to take it, "ONE DAY AT A TIME!!!"   *(unknown)*

King Heroin

King Heroin is my shepherd, I shall always want.
He makes me lie down in the gutter.
He leads me beside the troubled waters.
He destroys my soul.
He leads me in the paths of wickedness.
Yea, I shall walk through the Valley of Poverty and will fear no evil
For thou, Heroin, are with me.
Your needle and your capsule comfort me.
You strip the table of groceries in the presence of my family.
You rob my head of reason.
Surely heroin addiction shall stalk me all the days of my life,
And I will dwell in the house of the damned forever.

Anonymous 23rd Psalm Innovation; found beside the body of a suicide victim along with a note that said, "Jail didn't cure me. Nor did hospitalization help me for long. The doctor told my family it would have been better, and indeed kinder, if the person who got me hooked on dope had taken a gun and blown my brains out. And I wish to God he had. My God, how I wish it."

Rejoice in Recovery 12-Step Faith-Based Study
Participant's Lesson
Step #10   Date _____
"For I know the plans I have for you," says the Lord.
"They are plans for good and not for disaster, to give you a future and a hope."
Jeremiah 29: 11

<u>***Step #10 Smart Start:**</u>   *Devotionals Start on Page 45 LRB*

*Step #10:   Daily Inventory

We continued to take _____ inventory, and

when we were _____, _____ admitted it.

*Step #10 Paraphrase: *Accept that I'm human and will screw up.*
                                          Fix mistakes immediately.

*Step #10 Key Terms: *admit, determination, perseverance, reprieve, wield*

*Step #10 Chant:

*A clean slate (2X)	*This **new day** will be just great!*	*(paper/board)*
*Oops, a wrong (2X)	*I must fix it, not wait long*	*(write wrongs)*
*End my day (2X)	*Wipe all my mistakes away!*	*(tear up/erase)*
*Look my best!	*Do my best!*	
Be my best!	*God does the rest!*	

<u>***Step #10 Introduction:**</u> ***One Day at a Time***   *(based on AA; NA; 12/12; Beattie)*

*Daily Devotions: ***Start Your Day in a God-Focused Way:***
                                          The Peanut Butter & Jelly Approach to Life

Peanut butter and jelly *(PB n' J)* have long been essential staples in the American diet. They are also essential on the road to recovery. *PB n' J* writing helps you to learn from your past, live in the present, and look forward to your future. *PB n' J* writing includes:

P – **P**rayer & Praise
B - **B**ible Study
J - **J**ournaling

Daily Journal Entries:	*Short Personal Example:*
Bible Verse-for-the-Day:	* *Bible Verse-for-the-Day:*
Meditation/memorization verse from:	_____
*Daily Bible reading *(see Step #11 for ideas)*	_____
*Daily devotion *(e.g., those in The LR Bible)*	_____
*Collection of favorite Bible verses	_____
Prayer Requests:	*Prayer Requests:*_____
Who/what do I want to talk to God about today?	_____
Gratitude: What am I thankful for today?	**Gratitude:* _____
Growth: What did I allow God to teach me today?	**Growth:* _____
What good did I do for others today?	_____
Grouches: What mistakes did I make today?	**Grouches:* _____
How did I fix these mistakes today?	_____
Greats: What positive characteristics	**Greats:* _____
did I exhibit today?	_____

**Note: *You may choose to make these entries at the end of each day.*

Today's Daily Decisions
*Daily Determination: Today's Fruit of the Spirit   *(Galatians 5: 22-23 p. 1505)*
*Today I will demonstrate **love** by _____
*Today I will have **joy** because _____
*Today I will have **peace** because _____
*Today I will have **patience** with _____
*Today I will show **kindness** by _____
*Today I will demonstrate **goodness** by _____
*Today I will show **faithfulness** by _____
*Today I will show **gentleness** by _____
*Today I will demonstrate **self-control** about _____

---

*Daily Deceptions: The Temptation of Sensory Stimulation – *Steps #4 & #5*
*Today I will **not look** at _____
*Today I will **not listen** to _____
*Today I will **not lust** for _____

*Daily Distractions: BARFS - *Steps #4 & #5*
*Today I will **not be <u>b</u>itter** about _____
*Today I will **not be <u>a</u>ngry** about _____
*Today I will **not be <u>r</u>ebellious** about _____
*Today I will **not have <u>f</u>ear** about _____
*Today I will **not destroy myself** by **<u>s</u>elf-sabotage** *(hurting myself <u>m</u>entally, <u>e</u>motionally, <u>s</u>ocially, and <u>s</u>piritually)* such as: _____

---

*Daily Deliverance: Character Defects - *Steps #6 & #7*
*Today I give God my **addiction-related thoughts** about _____
*Today I give God my **sexually-related thoughts** about _____
*Today I give God my **money-related thoughts** about _____

*Daily Defense: Amends: to You, You to Me, To Myself - *Steps #8 & #9*
*Today I give up my **I-O-U Amends** excuses and ask forgiveness from _____
*Today I give up my **U-O-Me Amends** and forgive _____
*Today I make **I-O-Myself Amends** and forgive myself for _____

---

*Daily Determination: LOOK at Today in My New Way – *Step #10*
*Today I will be **honest** because _____
*Today I will ask for **help** when _____
*Today I will have **hope** because _____
*Today I will have **God-approved actions** such as: _____

---

*Today I will have **God-approved attitudes** such as: _____

---

*Step #10 Memory Verse: *Ephesians 6: 10-11 (p. 1517)*
>   Be **strong** in the Lord and in His mighty **power**.
>   **Put on all** of God's **armor**
>   so that you will be able to stand **firm** against **all** strategies of the **devil**.

1.   What strategies has Satan used to get you to do what he wanted you to do? _____
        _____
        _____

2.   I have practiced writing this verse on the margins of this page and other pages in
        the homework _____ times and know this verse from memory. _____
                                                                        Signature

*Step #10 Extra Credit Verse: *Psalm 118: 24 (p. 763)*
>   This is the **day** that the **Lord** has made.
>   We will **rejoice** and be **glad** in it.

1.   What are some of the advantages of turning my will and my life over to God at
        the beginning of each new day?
        *   *
        *   *

2.   I have practiced writing this verse on the margins of this page and other pages in
        the homework _____ times and know this verse from memory. _____
                                                                        Signature

*Step #10 Extra, Extra Credit For-Fun Verse: *Ephesians 4: 26-27 (p. 1514)*
        Paul reminds us,
>   Don't **sin** by letting **anger** control you.
>   Don't let the **sun** go **down** while you are still **angry**,
>   For **anger** gives a **foothold** to the **devil**.

1.   What happens over time if you *stuff-down* anger and refuse to deal with it?
        *
        *

*Step #10: Bible Stories:
        Beware: I Am Armed and Dangerous   *Ephesians 6 (pp. 1517-1518)*
        Behold: I Once Was Blind BUT Now I See   *Mark 10: 46-52 (p. 1269)*

*Enemy: *Ephesians 6: 10-12 (p. 1517)*
1.   Why are you supposed to **put on all** of the armor?

2.   What is the enemy's purpose?   What is Jesus purpose?
                (Hint: to answer fill-in-the-blanks see John 10: 10 p. 1358)
        The thief's (Satan's) purpose is to _____ and _____ and _____.
        My (Jesus') purpose is to give them (you) a _____ and _____ life.

3.   If you put on all of your armor, what will your status be at the end of the battle?
        (Hint: see verse 13)

*Equipment: *Ephesians 6: 13-17 (p. 1517)*
        *Fill-in-the-information on **The 12-Step Armor-of-God Pyramid***

Step *Write out wording for each step:*	Piece of Equipment *Draw pictures for each piece of equipment:*	Proverbs' Position *Write out scripture verses:*
Step #12: Sharing & Caring	Sword of the Spirit	Proverbs 4: 20-21 (p. 792)
Step #11: Prayer & Meditation	Prayer	Proverbs 2: 3 (p. 788)
Step #10: Daily Inventory	Shield of Faith	Proverbs 30: 5 (p. 819)
Step #8: Fence-Mending List Step #9: Fence-Mending Action	Shoes of Peace	Proverbs 4: 25-26 (p. 792)
Step #6: I Surrender. Step #7: Retrain Brain	Body Armor of God's Righteousness	Proverbs 4: 23 (p. 792)
Step#4: In-depth Inventory Step #5: Admit 3	Belt of Truth	Proverbs 12: 22 (p. 799)
Step #1: I can't. Step #2: God can. Step #3: I'll let Him. *(Base of pyramid; build up from)*	Helmet of Salvation	Proverbs 4: 13 (p. 791)

*Equipment: Put On or Leave Off?
  *Share **personal examples** when answering the following questions
  *Do you need more information about each piece of armor? If so,
   look at *The 12-Step Armor-of-God Pyramid on page 86.*

*<u>Step #12</u>: What has happened to you in the past when you **didn't** wield *(use)* the
sword of the spirit? _____ ____ _____
*What will happen to you today when you **do** wield *(use)* the **sword of the spirit**? _____

_____

*<u>Step #11</u>: Prayer: *not listed as a piece of armor but essential in battle*
*What has happened to you in the past when you **didn't pray** for God's will to be done?

_____
*What will happen to you **today** when you **do pray** for God's will be done? _____

_____

*<u>Step #10</u>: What has happened to you in the past when you **didn't** put up the **shield of
faith**? _____
*What will happen to you today when you **do** put up the **shield up faith**? _____

_____

*<u>Steps #8 & #9</u>: What has happened to you in the past when you **didn't** put on the **shoes
of peace**? _____ ____ _____
*What will happen to you today when you **do** put on the **shoes of peace**? _____

_____

*<u>Steps #6 & #7</u>: What has happened to you in the past when you **didn't** put on the **body
armor of God's righteousness**? _____ ____ _____
*What will happen to you today when you **do** put on the **body armor of God's
righteousness**? _____

*<u>Steps #4 & #5</u>: What has happened to you in the past when you **didn't** put on the **belt
of truth**? _____ ____ _____
*What will happen to you today when you **do** put on the **belt of truth**? _____

_____

*<u>Steps #1, #2, & #3</u>: What has happened to you in the past when you **didn't** put on the
helmet of salvation? _____ ____ _____
*What will happen to you today when you **do** put on the **helmet of salvation**? _____

_____

*Energy: *Ephesians 6: 18-20 (p. 1517)*
1. What are some of the guidelines for prayer that Paul gives?
   *   *
   *   *
   *   *
   *   *

*Behold: I Once Was Blind, BUT Now I See
Jesus Heals Blind Bartimaeus (B)   *Mark 10: 46-52 (p. 1269)*

As a soldier, once you have put on all of your armor and are ready for battle, you have to be able to **see** the enemy *face-to-face*. If you **can't see**, you **can't fight**.

Bartimaeus	**Me**
*How did **B** irritate the crowd	*What do I do that irritates others?
*What did **B** ask Jesus for and why?	*What do I ask Jesus for and why?
*When told to shut up, what did **B** do?	*When told to shut up, what do I do?
*When Jesus called him, what did **B** do? * * *	*When Jesus calls me, what do I do?
*When Jesus asked **B**, "What do you want me to do for you? what was **B** response?	*When Jesus asks, "What do you want me to do for you?" what is my response?
*Why did Jesus heal **B**?	*What are you willing to do to help Jesus help you?
*What did **B** do after being healed?	*What will I do after Jesus helps me?

*Step #10: Did You Get It?   *(based on AA; NA; 12/12; Beattie; Hall)*
Please circle True or False, and **explain why** you made each choice:

1.   I must admit when I am wrong and fix the problem
          immediately.   True   False

2.   If I choose to use, I won't lose.   True   False

3.   Since I'm frustrated and angry right now, it will be better if
          I deal with this problem tomorrow.   True   False

4.   When I'm about to make a mistake, I should immediately
          stop, look, admit, and correct.   True   False

5.   Forgiven people, forgive people.   True   False

6.   When I am cocky about how well I'm doing,
        I may be in danger of relapse.   True   False

7.   When I'm angry, I always have a good reason for being angry.   True   False

8.   My resentments do not impact my daily life.   True   False

9.   I am always in the process of recovery. I am never recovered.   True   False

10.   When I have a problem, I should ask for help even though
        asking for help is not easy for me to do.   True   False

*BEWARE: AA/NA teach that we should never, ever put ourselves in situations
        where we are too **h**ungry, too **a**ngry, too **l**onely, or too **t**ired. In other
        words, HALT! when you find yourself in the following situations:

Situation Today:
What might happen if I'm too **H**ungry? _____
What might happen if I'm too **A**ngry? _____
What might happen if I'm too **L**onely? _____
What might happen if I'm too **T**ired? _____

*<u>Step #10 Reflections</u>:
1.   Today I Will Have **JOY**. I will focus **on J**esus, **O**thers, **and Y**ou *(myself)*.
        The two commandments Jesus gave us are: (1) you must love the Lord your **God**
        with all your heart, all your soul, and all your mind, and (2) love your **neighbor**
        as **yourself** *(Matthew 22: 37-40 p. 1232)*.

*<u>J</u> – Jesus: Today I will pray for God's will, not mine, to be done. Jesus modeled this
for me in *"The Lord's Prayer" (Matthew 6: 10, p. 1204)*.

Today I want God's will, not mine, to be done regarding: _____
_____

*<u>O</u> - Others: Today I will follow *"The Golden Rule," "Do to <u>others</u> whatever you would
like them to do to <u>you</u>," (Matthew 7: 12, p. 1206).*

Today I am going to help someone by: _____
_____

*<u>Y</u> – You: Jesus promised, *"Come unto me all of you who are weary and carry heavy
burdens, and I will give you rest (Matthew 11: 28, p. 1214).*

Today I am going to help myself by giving Jesus the following burdens: _____
_____

Then I am going to rest.

2. **Daily Knock-Me-Downs** *(KMD's)* **&** **Pick-Me-Ups** *(PMU's)*
        BUT: <u>B</u>ehold the <u>U</u>nderlying <u>T</u>ruth

Example:
I am tortured by drug-dreams
But when I wake up, I say my favorite Bible verses out-loud.

Paul's KMD's & PMU's:	*My Personal KMD's & PMU's:*
We are pressed on every side by troubles,	I am _____
BUT *we are not crushed and broken.*	BUT I _____
	_____
We are perplexed (confused, puzzled),	I am _____
BUT *we don't give up and quit.*	But I _____
	_____
We are hunted down,	I am _____
BUT *God never abandons us.*	But God _____
	_____
We get knocked down,	I get _____
BUT *we get up again and keep going*	But I _____
2 Corinthians 4: 8-9 (p. 1484)	_____

3. **Daily Planner:** Writing down AA/NA/12-step faith-based meetings, appointments, and places I need to go on a calendar in a daily planner helps me organize each day in a meaningful way. As I look at my personal calendar I can see: (1) where I am (2) where I've been, and (3) where I'm going.
Advantages of writing a daily agenda about what I'm going to do today are:
*
*
* _____

Please complete the following check sheet during the week:

Name _____
Dates: _____
Class/Church Attendance

Date:	Class/Church Name:
_____	_____
_____	_____
_____	_____
_____	_____
_____	_____

_____ Class
_____ Brought Bible/Pencil
_____ Brought Extra Credit
_____ Brought Journal

Memory Practice Step #10
_____ Step # 10
_____ Memory Verse
_____ Extra Cr. Memory Verse

Devotions begin on p. 45	Bible Reading	Homework for Step #10
_____ Devotional #1	_____ Day #1	_____ Day #1
_____ Devotional #2	_____ Day #2	_____ Day #2
_____ Devotional #3	_____ Day #3	_____ Day #3
_____ Devotional #4	_____ Day #4	_____ Day #4
_____ Devotional #5	_____ Day #5	_____ Day #5
_____ Devotional #6	_____ Day #6	_____ Day #6
_____ Devotional #7	_____ Day #7	_____ Day #7

Please write your prayer requests below:

STTA: **Poem: I Am Meth**   *(Anonymous: Written by a meth addict while in jail)*

I destroy homes: I tear families apart.
I take your children, and that's just the start.
I'm more costly than diamonds, more precious than gold,
The sorrow I bring is a sight to behold.

      If you need me, remember I'm easily found.
      I live all around you - in schools and in town.
      I live with the rich; I live with the poor.
      I live down the street, and maybe next door.

I'm made in a lab but not like you think.
I can be made under the kitchen sink,
In your child's closet, and even in the woods.
If this scares you to death, well it certainly should.

      I have many names, but there's one you know best.
      I'm sure you've heard of me; my name's crystal meth.
      My power is awesome; try me, you'll see.
      But if you do, you may never break free.

Just try me once, and I might let you go,
But try me twice, and I'll own your soul.
When I possess you, you'll steal, and you'll lie.
You do what you have to - just to get high.

      The crimes you'll commit for my narcotic charms,
      Will be worth the pleasure you'll feel in your arms.
      You'll lie to your mother; you'll steal from your dad.
      When you see their tears, you should feel sad.

But you'll forget your morals and how you were raised.
I'll be your conscience; I'll teach you my ways.
I take kids from parents, and parents from kids.
I turn people from God and separate friends.

      I'll take everything from you - your looks and your pride.
      I'll be with you always - right by your side.
      You'll give up everything - your family, your home.
      Your friends, your money, and you'll be alone.

I'll take and take, till you have nothing more to give.
When I'm finished with you, you'll be lucky to live.
If you try me be warned - this is no game.
If given the chance, I'll drive you insane.

      I'll ravish your body; I'll control your mind.
      I'll own you completely; your soul will be mine.
      The nightmares I'll give you while lying in bed.
      The voices you'll hear, from inside your head.

The sweats, the shakes, the visions you'll see.
I want you to know, these are all gifts from me.
But then it's too late, and you'll know in your heart,
That you are mine, and we shall not part.

      You'll regret that you tried me; they always do,
      But you came to me, not I to you.
      You knew this would happen; many times you were told.
      But you challenged my power, and chose to be bold.

You could have said, "No!" and just walked away.
If you could live that day over, now what would you say?
I'll be your master; you will be my slave.
I'll even go with you, when you go to your grave.

      Now that you have met me, what will you do? Will you try me or not? It's all up to you.
      I can bring you more misery than words can tell. Come take my hand; let me lead you to hell.

Rejoice in Recovery 12-Step Faith-Based Study
Participant's Lesson
Step #11   Date _____
"For I know the plans I have for you," says the Lord.
"They are plans for good and not for disaster, to give you a future and a hope."
Jeremiah 29: 11

*Smart Step Start
*Step #11:   Prayer & Meditation   *Devotionals Start on Page 419 LRB*

We sought through _____ and _____   *(How)*
to improve our _____ _____ with _____   *(Goal)*
Praying _____ for   *(What)*
knowledge of _____ _____ for us   *(Whose will)*
and the_____ to carry that out.   *(Help needed)*

*Step #11 Paraphrase: *Ask God to show me how to live.*
*Step #11 Key Terms: *conscious contact, compromise, contemplate, meditate*

*Step #11 Chant: *I must pray. I must pray. I must talk **with** God each day.*
                          Of God's love I am assured when I read His Holy Word.

*Step #11 Introduction: *Is **God a Genie in a Bottle/Lamp?***

1.   Approximately how many minutes do you spend in **prayer** each day? _____

       How many of these minutes are spent **asking** God for something? _____

2.   What is **prayer**?

3.   How is prayer going to increase your **conscious**, deliberate
       on-purpose, **contact** with God?

4.   What are some examples of who/what you pray about?
       *   *
       *   *
       *   *

5.   **Prayer** includes:
                                          Personal prayer examples:

*P-Praising   Gratitude!   What He does _____
*R-Repenting: Grouches!   What I did… _____
*A-Asking: Give me!   What I want…_____
*Y-Yielding: Growth!   What He wants _____

6.   How can you **improve** your prayer life?
       *

       *

7.   When you **pray** and **ask** God for something, He always hears and answers His
      children, **but** He doesn't always answer, "Yes." Share personal examples:

God's Answer: *What you asked for:*

*Yes   * _____

*No   * _____

*Wait   * _____

*I have something   * _____
  better for you   _____

8.   Paul reminds us: *Examples in my life of:*

Always be *joyful*.   *Joy: _____

Never stop *praying*.   **Prayer:* _____

Be *thankful* in all circumstances,   **Bad times:* _____

for this is God's *will* for you   **Good times:* _____

who *belong* to Christ.   **How I know I belong to Christ:* _____

1 Thessalonians 5: 16-17 (p. 1542)   _____

9.   When you **meditate**, you:

             ***Concentrate** on just one thing

             ***Empty** your mind of competing thoughts, and

             ***Contemplate** the meaning for your life

      What are some **topics** you can meditate on that will **improve** your **relationship**
      with God and draw you **closer** to Him?

      *   *

      *   *

      *   *

10.   How will **meditation** on Bible verses **improve** your **relationship** with God and
      draw you closer to Him?

11.   Approximately how many minutes do you spend reading your **Bible** each day? ___

*What time of the day do you read your **Bible**? _____

*What are some advantages of using a ***read-the-Bible-through-in-a-year plan***?_____

_____

*If you memorize a ***verse-a-week*** for a year, how many verses would you know? _____

*There are 31 chapters in **Proverbs**. Every month you could read a ***chapter-a-day***.
Today's proverb chapter is chapter number ___. Write your favorite verse from this
proverb: _____

_____

*When you are down-in-the-dumps, there are many ***pick-me-up verses*** in **Psalms**.
Write a favorite verse from Psalms: _____

_____

12.   The **Bible** contains

God's: *What **changes** should you make in your daily Bible reading?*

B-Basic   _____

I- Instructions   _____

B-Before   _____

L-Leaving   _____

E-Earth   _____

13.   You are trying to make a **decision**. How will you discover **God's will**?

****A**-Ask: What does **God** have to say? **Pray!**

****B**-Bible: What does the **Bible** have to say? **Study!**

****C**-Conscience: What does my **conscience** have to say? **Meditate!**

****D**-Determination: Am I making a *well-thought-out, **stick-to-it*** decision?

****E**-Empower: Will God **empower** me to do this?

****F**-Follow: Who will I **follow**? What would Jesus do?

I need to make a decision about: _____

*What do I think **God** is going to say? _____

*What does my **Bible** say?   _____

*What does my **conscience** say? _____

*Proof of **determination** to stick with my decision: _____

*How is God going to **empower** me to do this? _____

*Who am I **following** in making this decision? _____

*Step #11 Memory Verse: *Psalm 119: 11 (p. 763)*   **Draw your heart*

*I have hidden your **word** in my **heart**,*   *w/God's word inside:*

that I might not **sin** against you.

1.   How do you get God's word into your heart? _____

How will His word help you?_____

2.   I have practiced writing this verse on the margins of this page and other pages in

the homework _____ times and know this verse from memory. _____

Signature

*Step #11 Extra Credit Verse: *Philippians 4: 6-7 (p. 1525)*   **Draw a*

*Don't **worry** about **anything**;*   *peaceful you:*

*instead **pray** about **everything**.*

*Tell **God** what you **need**,*

*and **thank** Him for all He has **done**.*

*Then you will experience God's **peace**.*

*which exceeds anything we can **understand**.*

*His **peace** will guard your **hearts** and **minds** as you live in Christ Jesus.*

1.   How can **I know** *that I know* **that I know** that I have God's peace in my heart

and life? _____

_____

2.   I have practiced writing this verse on the margins of this page and other pages in

the homework _____ and know this verse from memory. _____

Signature

*Step #11 Bible Story: Dare to be a Daniel
Daniel Chapters 1-6 (pp. 1073- 1085); Biography (p. 1075)

*Chapter 1: Captivating Captives *(pp. 1074-1076)*

1.   Daniel, Shadrach, Meshach, and Abednego were taken from their hometown *(Jerusalem)* and moved to Babylon. What **positive character traits** made them top choices to be captives *(slaves, prisoners)*?
          *Look like outside: _____
          *Look like inside: _____

2.   What kind of **brainwashing** did King Nebuchadnezzar order these captives to receive?
          *Education: _____
          *Nutrition: _____

3.   What **boundaries** did the men have regarding the food the king's men, *their frenemies,* asked them to eat?

4.   What **boundaries** do I need to establish in my life?
          *
          *
          *
          *
          *

*Chapter 3: Fiery-Furnace-Faith *(pp. 1078-1080)*

1.   Look at the wide variety of musical instruments that were used *(see verse 5)*.
      *How does the devil use music today to lead us astray?
      _____

      *How does God use music? _____
      _____

2.   When Shadrach, Meshach, and Abednego faced a gold statue 90 feet tall and 9 feet wide, they had the following **choices** and **consequences** to consider:
          *Bad Choice: _____   *Consequence:_____
          *Good Choice: _____   *Consequence:_____

3.   What were the men's verbal responses to their *face-the-furnace* **choice**?
          *
          *
          *

4.   After Shadrach, Meshach, and Abednego were tied up and thrown into the furnace that was 7 times hotter than usual, what did King Nebuchadnezzar see that surprised him?

5.   What was the evidence that God had protected these men from the fire?
        *
        *
        *

6.   Application: Do you have **fiery-furnace-faith**? What kinds of *fiery-furnace trials n' tribulations* have you been going through where God will rescue you - if you let Him?
        My fiery-furnace trials n' tribulations: *How God can help me if I let Him:*

        *   *

        *   *

        *   *

*Chapter 4: Tree-Dream Disaster *(pp. 1081-1082)*

1.   What kind of **insane** life was King Nebuchadnezzar going to live if he didn't heed the *tree-dream* warning and **choose-to-change**?
        *   *
        *   *
        *   *

2.   What advice did Daniel give King Nebuchadnezzar concerning the **good choices** he should make? *Hint: see verse 27 for part of the answer*
        *   *
        *   *

3.   What did the king do when his **sanity** returned?
        *
        *
        *

4.   Application: Share times of **insanity** in your life.
        What happened?   *How did/are you going to get your **sanity** back?*
        *   *

        *   *

        *   *

5.   King Nebuchadnezzar had a **humbling experience**. Share a humbling experience in your life in which God is teaching you **changes** you need to make. God may also be letting you know what the **consequences** are going to be if you **choose** to continue down the path you are on. *Hint: see Footnote 4: 18-27 p. 1080*

*Chapter 5: Beware the Fingers/Hand Writing-on-the-Wall! *(pp. 1082-1084)*
Note: New King, Belshazzar; same Daniel (about 82 years old)
City had high walls. Even though surrounded by their enemy, the people
thought they were safe. Are we ever safe from our enemy, the devil?

1.   What happened during the party King Belshazzar gave that terrified him?

2.   King Belshazzar knew what had happened to King Nebuchadnezzar. He knew he
      had **choices** about how to live his life, yet he chose to **ignore** the **consequences**.
      What were his choices and the consequence for each?
      *Bad Choice: _____   *Consequence: _____
      *Good Choice:_____   *Consequence: _____

3.   What might God write on the wall of your cell/room that would get your
      attention?

4.   King Belshazzar waited until it was **too late to change**. What happens if we wait
      until it is too late to change? *Hint: see Footnote 5: 18-31 p. 1083*

5.   What have you learned from your past that can help you in the present and have a
      positive impact on your future?

Life-Lessons Learned from Past:	Help for Present:	Impact on Future:
*	*	*
*	*	*
*	*	*

*Chapter 6: Daniel in the Lion's Den *(pp. 1084-1085)*
Note: New King, Darius; same Daniel

1.   **Liars:** Who were the liars?_____
      *What was their problem? _____
      *Explain how some of your frenemies have the same problem. *Hint: see footnote*
      6: 1-4 p. 1084 _____
      _____

2.   **Law:** What law did the liars convince King Darius to make? _____
      _____

3.   **Listen:** What choices did Daniel have, and what were the consequences?
      *Bad Choice: _____*Consequence: _____
      *Good Choice: _____*Consequence: _____

4.   **Look for a loop-hole:** Daniel could have closed his window and **prayed**.
      What did Daniel do?   Why didn't Daniel **compromise**?
      *   *

5.   What do we know about Daniel's prayer life? *Hint: see verses 10 & 11*

6.   **Lion Lunch**: What happened to Daniel when he was thrown into the lions' den?

7.   **Liberated:** Daniel developed a great relationship with God **long before** he was thrown into the lion's den?
       *How good is **your relationship** with God? _____
       _____
       *What are you doing to **improve** this relationship? _____
       _____

8.   **Long-Before:** Daniel had well-developed **prayer habits** long before he ended-up in the lions' den. Considering that there may be some **lions looming** in your future, what **changes** should you make in your own prayer life?
       *

       *

       *

*Step #11: Did You Get It?

*Please circle True or False, and **explain why** you made each choice:
(based on AA; NA; 12/12)

1.   I know what's best for my family, so God should listen to me and take care of them my way.   True   False

2.   When I **pray**, I should ask for my will to be accomplished.   True   False

3.   If I **pray** only when I am hurting, I will have fewer hurting times.   True   False

4.   God will provide **prayer power** for me whether or not I ask.   True   False

5.   My **prayer-life** will get better and better as I pray more and more.   True   False

6.   When God's will for me becomes my will for me, I am well on my way to a **spiritual awakening** *(Step #12).*   True   False

7.   Basically **prayer** is a 911 call that should be used only in times of emergency.   True   False

8.   As I go through the day, when I become irritated, frustrated, and exasperated, I should **pray** repeatedly, "Your will be done."   True   False

*<u>Step #11 Reflections</u>: Daniel faced lions that could have destroyed him. He was prepared long before he faced those lions. You need to be prepared to face the lions-in-your-life - lions who are lurking and ready to lunge!

Take-a-look at some lions in your life:
Lion #1: Loneliness
Example from my life:
*

Lion #2: Shame
Example from my life:
*

Lion #3: Despair
Example from my life:
*

Lion #4: Suicidal Thoughts
Example from my life:
 •

Lion #5: _____
    (other)

Write verse. God's "lion-licking" promises:
*Hebrews 13: 5

*Psalm 32: 5

*Psalm 42: 5

*Psalm 94: 17

*Select & write a Bible verse:

Please complete the following check sheet during the week:

Name _____
Dates: _____
Class/Church Attendance
Date: Class/Church Name:

_____   _____
_____   _____
_____   _____
_____   _____
_____   _____

_____ Class
_____ Brought Bible/Pencil
_____ Brought Extra Credit
_____ Brought Journal

Memory Practice Step #11
_____ Step #11
_____ Memory Verse
_____ Extra Cr. Memory Verse

Devotions begin on p. 419
_____ Devotional #1
_____ Devotional #2
_____ Devotional #3
_____ Devotional #4
_____ Devotional #5
_____ Devotional #6
_____ Devotional #7

Bible Reading
_____ Day #1
_____ Day #2
_____ Day #3
_____ Day #4
_____ Day #5
_____ Day #6
_____ Day #7

Homework for Step # 11
_____ Day #1
_____ Day #2
_____ Day #3
_____ Day #4
_____ Day #5
_____ Day #6
_____ Day #7

Please write your prayer requests below:

STTA: An Addict's Night Before Christmas   *(innovation)*

'Twas the night before Christmas and all through my life,
There was conflict and chaos, discouragement, strife.
My mistakes on display for the whole world to see.
What in the world will happen to me?

I tried to nestle down snug in my bed,
But the nightmares I had were something to dread:
The pain of addiction, the high - then the crash,
The lives I had ruined protecting my stash.

When at my heart's door, there arose such a clatter.
I flung the door open and screamed, "What's the matter?"
Then what in my open heart's door should appear?
The glory of God and His presence so near.

His son, Jesus Christ, confronted me now:
Face-to-face with my addiction, please help me somehow!
My **past** was a shambles. My **present** not right.
My **future,** a mess, unless I changed tonight.

He showed me a road, the road I'd been upon,
Where **choices** were bad, and **decisions** were wrong.
He asked, "Do you want to make everything right?
Then fall to your knees and accept me tonight.

Make a **U-Turn**. **Change** your direction in life.
Give me your agony, misery, and strife.
Let me be your **BOSS**. Let me show you the way.
Ask, "What would Jesus do?" throughout every day.   *(WWJD)*

You've a **choice**-do you want to continue your plight?
Or do you want a **NEW LIFE** beginning tonight?"
I paused, and I pondered, can I give this stuff up:
The medication;* the money;** the men *(woMen)* who're corrupt?

Can I ask God's forgiveness for all that I've done:
The using, the drinking, the *sexing*, the *fun*?
I stopped, dropped, and prayed confessing it all,
"Oh God, please forgive me. I give **YOU** my **ALL**!"

I stood! Then I shouted! I praised Christ, my King!
My Savior! My Lord! My All! Everything!
Happy birthday to Jesus! Happy birthday to me!
My gift to Him? What? I'm giving Him **ME**!

(Note: *Medication-representative of all drugs; **Money-representative of all illegal means to obtain)

Rejoice in Recovery 12-Step Faith-Based Study
Participant's Lesson
Step #12   Date: _____

"For I know the plans I have for you," says the Lord.
"They are plans for good and not for disaster, to give you a future and a hope. "Jeremiah 29:11

*Step #12 Smart Start: *Devotionals start on page 917 LRB*

*Step #12:   Sharing & Caring

Having had a _____ _____ as the result of these steps, *(Had what?)*

we try to _____ this message to _____   *(Do what?)*

and to _____ these principles in all our affairs.   *(Live how?)*

*Step #12 Paraphrase: *Keep doing Steps 1-11, and pass it on. Be a blessing to others.*

*Step #12 Key Terms: *attention intervention, spiritual awakening*

*Step #12 Chant:

I was blind. I could not see. Jesus laid His hands on me.
Wide-open eyes, I see the light. Now I'm doing each step right.
Give God my will. Give Him my life. Give Him all my pain and strife.
Secure in God's arms. He will keep me safe from harm.
Now I have a 12-step plan. Reach up to God! Reach out to man!

*Step #12 Introduction: A Journey on Recovery Road Leads to Spiritual Discovery

1.   The following are some indicators of a **spiritual awakening**.

*Indicator: **Evidence in my life:*

*God grabbed me! _____

*I paid attention! _____

*God's in the driver's seat of my life! _____

*I'm traveling in the right direction! _____

2.   As you begin your journey on the **Road to Recovery**, you need to **search** your heart while making decisions regarding:

S-Seeking a Sponsor & a Support Group

Why should you have a sponsor you call everyday? _____
_____

E-Evaluating Each and Every Decision

Why should you carefully evaluate each and every decision? _____
_____

A-Attending Meetings

Why should you attend 90 meetings in 90 days? _____
_____

R-Really Reading Your Bible Daily

How are you going to get the most benefit from your Bible study? _____
_____

C-Carefully Choosing a Church & Attending Weekly

What are you going to look for in a church? _____
_____

H-Having Honest & Heart-Healthy Habits

How are you going to prove to friends and family that they can **really trust** you
this time?_____

3. While traveling the **Road to Recovery**, you have made a lot progress. However, at times there are some potential potholes that you may need to deal with. For example:

Step #1: **A**dmit my life is a wreck
    Progress: _____
    Potential Potholes: _____

Step #2: **B**elieve God can help me
    Progress: _____
    Potential Potholes: _____

Step #3: **C**hoose God as my boss
    Progress: _____
    Potential Potholes: _____

Step #4: **D**etail my moral mistakes
    Progress: _____
    Potential Potholes: _____

Step #5: **E**xplain my moral mistakes to God, me, and someone else
    Progress: _____
    Potential Potholes: _____

Step #6: **F**inally face my faults and fears
    Progress: _____
    Potential Potholes: _____

Step #7: **G**ive God the go-ahead to remove bad habits
    Progress: _____
    Potential Potholes: _____

Step #8: **H**ave a list of those I've harmed
    Progress: _____
    Potential Potholes: _____

Step #9: **I**nitiate, start making, amends
    Progress: _____
    Potential Potholes: _____

Step #10: **J**ust take *one-day-at-a-time*
    Progress: _____
    Potential Potholes: _____

Step #11: **K**eep on praying and studying my Bible
    Progress: _____
    Potential Potholes: _____

Step #12: **L**ead others to a new life with God
    Progress: _____
    Potential Potholes: _____

4.   **How** do you **benefit** when you **help others**?
    *
    *

5.   Who are you going to **help**?   How are you going to **help** them?
    *   *
    *   *

*Step #12 Memory Verse: *John 5: 6b (p. 1348)*
>   *Would **you** like to get **well**?*
1.   How do I demonstrate to God that I really want to get well? _____
_____

2. I have practiced writing this verse on the margins of this page and other pages in the homework _____ times and know this verse from memory. _____
Signature

Step #12 Extra Credit Verse: *2 Timothy 1: 7 (p. 1561)*
>   *For **God** has **not** given us a spirit of*
>   ***fear and timidity** but of*
>   ***power**,*
>   ***love**, and*
>   ***self-discipline.** (a sound mind).*

The Wizard of Oz application:
*Lion seeks courage
*Tin Man seeks a new heart
*Scarecrow seeks a new brain

1.   Which character in the *Wizard of Oz* are you the most like and why? _____
_____

2.   I have practiced writing this verse on the margins of this page and other pages in the homework _____ times and know this verse from memory. _____
Signature

*Step #12 Bible Stories: Trilogy: Help Myself! Help a Friend! Help a Stranger!
>   **Help Myself:*   The Lame Man at the Pool *John 5: 1-15 (pp. 1347-1348)*
>   **Help a Friend:*   Jesus Heals a Paralyzed Man *Mark 2: 1-12 (pp. 1252-1253)*
>   **Help a Stranger:*   The Good Samaritan *Luke 10: 25-37 (pp. 1308-1309)*

*Help Myself: The Lame Man at the Pool *John 5: 1-15 (pp. 1347-1348); Devotional p. 1347*
>   ***To Change or Not to Change? It Is My Choice!***

Lame Man	**Me**
*What **question** did Jesus ask the lame man? **	*What **question** does Jesus ask me? **
*What were the man's **excuses** for not getting well? ** **	*What were/are my **excuses** for not getting clean/sober? ** **
*What did Jesus tell the man to **do**? ** ** **	*What is Jesus telling me to **do**? ** ** **
*What did Jesus tell the man to **stop doing**? **	*What did/does Jesus tell me to **stop doing?** **
*Consequence if he **didn't change**? **	*Consequence if I **don't change**? **

*Help a Friend: Jesus Heals a Paralyzed Man: *Mark 2: 1-12 (pp. 1252-1253)*
(Some things you can't fix, BUT you can take them to Jesus. Source: Unknown)

Paralyzed Man	**Me**
*What was the man's **problem**? **	*What is my **problem**? **
*How did his friends **help** him? **	*How can my friends **help** me? **
*What **problems** did the friends encounter? ** ** **	*What **problems** do my friends encounter when trying to help me? ** **
*How did Jesus **help** the man? ** **	*How can Jesus **help** me? ** **
*Who had **faith** that Jesus could heal the man? *(Hint: their faith)* ** **	*Who has **faith** that Jesus can heal me? *(Hint: family, friends)* ** **
*What did Jesus tell the man **to do** after he was healed? ** ** **	*What does Jesus want me **to do** after I am healed? ** ** **

*Beware! Why **shouldn't** you reach out to help a *"frenemy"?*
        **

        **

*Help a Stranger: The Good Samaritan *Luke 10: 25-37 (pp. 1308-1309; Footnote p. 1308)*
Introduction: Challenge to Jesus
1.   What was the first question the religious expert asks Jesus?
        *

2.   What did Moses' law say you must do to receive eternal life?
        *
        *

3.   What was the second question the religious expert asks Jesus?
        *

Response: Story (Note: Story takes place on a lonely, dangerous road between Jerusalem and Jericho)

Man	**Me**
*What happened to the man who needed **help**? **	*What happened to me, so that I need **help**? **
**	**
**	**
*What **excuses** might the priest and temple assistant have used to justify not reaching out and helping the man? **	*What **excuses** do others use to justify not reaching out and helping me? **
**	**
**	**
***Excuses** the Good Samaritan could have used for not reaching out and helping the man? **	*What **excuses** do I use for not reaching out and helping others? **
**	**
**	**
*Why did the despised Samaritan **reach out** and help the man? **	*Why should I **reach out** and help others? **
**	**
*How did the despised Samaritan **reach out** and help the man? **	*How can I **reach out** and help others? **
**	**
**	**

The End: Jesus Answers the Challenge

1. Jesus' confrontational question to the religious expert was, "Now which of these three would you say was a neighbor to the man who was attacked by bandits?"
   What was the expert's response? _____
   What did Jesus tell him to do? _____
2. What does "The Good Samaritan Story" **teach me** about Step #12?
   * _____
   * _____

*Step #12: Did You Get It?

Fill out the following outline in preparation for sharing your story with others:

_____**Personal Story**

(your name)

1.   What happened in my past?   *(Note: no down and dirty details)*
      *

      *

2.   Why did I start using drugs?   How did my addiction begin?
      *

      *

3.   What did my addiction cost me?
      *

      *

      *

4.   What kind of an attention intervention, *a stop, look, listen, choose-to-change experience,* did I have or do I need?
      *

      *

5.   What is God teaching me now?
      *

      *

      *

      *

6.   How am I going to reach out and demonstrate compassion and concern for others?
      *

      *

      *

      *

      *

7.   **I share because I care!** I shared my personal story with? _____:
      My sharing helped him/her in the following ways:
      *

      *

*Step #12 Reflections: **Stupid Choices: My Life Is a Mess!**
                                     Smart Choices: I'm on the Road to Success!

Allen Berger (2000) has identified twelve stupid choices you could make to mess up your recovery. The choices below incorporate many of his suggestions as well as those from others who have experienced the *ups-and-downs* of recovery. Beware the triggers and traps of relapse and focus on your triumphs as you make *smart choices* that contribute to progress on your journey of spiritual discovery.

For each ***stupid choice*** that follows, suggest an alternative, **a *smart choice***:

Stupid Choice #1: When I get out in the world, I need a **place to live**. Since I don't have anywhere else to go, I'll stay temporarily with my frenemies.
Smart Choice #1: _____

Stupid Choice #2: I don't need a new **support system** with a **sponsor, church,** and **new friends**. I can handle my recovery myself.
Smart Choice #2: _____

Stupid Choice #3: I don't need to attend **meetings** and **work** the **12-steps again**. I've already worked those steps once.
Smart Choice #3: _____

Stupid Choice #4: I'll just **use** drugs or **drink occasionally**. I know lots of people who do, and they are doing just fine.
Smart Choice #4: _____

Stupid Choice #5: I'll keep my **relapse** a **secret**. I'm embarrassed to let my new friends know that I've relapsed. I can **stop** using **on my own**
Smart Choice #5: _____

Stupid Choice #6: I'll stop using the drug I'm addicted to and **switch** to a **different drug**, one that I'm not addicted to.
Smart Choice #6: _____

Stupid Choice #7: I'll ask the doctor to give me a **prescription** for some **pills** for dental surgery, back pain, or to help me sleep. I need pills to deal with the pain.
Smart Choice #7: _____

Stupid Choice #8: When asked point-blank questions about my recovery, to avoid confrontation, I may be forced to be slightly **less-than-truthful**. Some things are best kept to oneself.
Smart Choice #8: _____

Stupid Choice #9: I am certainly **NOT** going to **ask** any of the people I know **for help**. Some people just want to make stupid suggestions that I certainly do not intend to follow.
Smart Choice #9: _____

Stupid Choice #10: When I get out in the world, I've got some **bills** I need to pay. Without a job there's only one way I know to make a **quick buck**.
Smart Choice #10: _____

Stupid Choice #11: I am ready **now** for a **new, romantic relationship**. I don't want to wait a year. My previous romantic relationships did not work because I was using.
Smart Choice #11: _____

Stupid Choice #12: Giving up my drug-of-choice and being sober is going to result in an **easy life**, *smooth sailing*. When using, I had to work hard and was relentless in my pursuit of drugs,
Smart Choice #12: _____

Summary: What are 4 ways I can use my heart hurts to help and give hope to others?
  ** _____
  ** _____
  ** _____
  ** _____

*Who did you share Step #12, the lame man, paralyzed man, and good Samaritan stories with? _____
*Reactions to sharing? _____
_____
_____

Please complete the following check sheet during the week:

Name _____   _____ Class
Dates: _____   _____ Brought Bible/Pencil
Class/Church Attendance   _____ Brought Extra Credit
Date: Class/Church Name: _____ Brought Journal

_____   _____
_____   _____   Memory Practice Step #12
_____   _____   _____ Step # 12
_____   _____   _____ Memory Verse
_____   _____ Extra Cr. Memory Verse

Devotions begin on p. 917   Bible Reading   Homework for Step # 12
_____ Devotional #1   _____ Day #1   _____ Day #1
_____ Devotional #2   _____ Day #2   _____ Day #2
_____ Devotional #3   _____ Day #3   _____ Day #3
_____ Devotional #4   _____ Day #4   _____ Day #4
_____ Devotional #5   _____ Day #5   _____ Day #5
_____ Devotional #6   _____ Day #6   _____ Day #6
_____ Devotional #7   _____ Day #7   _____ Day #7

Please write your prayer requests below:

STTA: Do I Like Who I Am?

Note: Inspired by my recovery house experiences; M. K., who struggled to decide whether to go to prison or a residential recovery program; and Green Eggs and Ham by Dr. Seuss (1960)

I do not like who I am!
I do not like me Sam-I-am.

I do not like it where I am! *(jail)*
This place here is not worth a _mmmm_!

The space in here is very tight.
The rules, I just can't get um right.

And I can never go outside,
Cause in my cell I must abide.

And don't ask me about the food,
Cause what I say would be so rude.

Day and night the doors go slam.
I do not like it where I am!

And then one day I get the news,
Now I have a chance to choose.

The choice the judge gives to me? *(choice)*
Prison, rehab, which will it be?

In prison, I'll not be free,   *(prison)*
For years, an eternity.

The rules will go on and on,
Until my sanity is gone.

I'll not be free to go outside,
With others there I may collide.

A rehab house, it's not so bad, *(rehab)*
Although, sometimes I may get mad.

Cause I'll have to do my chores,
And they may want me to do more:

Make my bed; sweep the floor;
Wash the dishes; wipe the door.

I'll have to watch my words, not cuss,
Or at me they will really fuss!

They may make me pay a fine,
For bad words, each and every time.

Meetings will seem to never end.
We'll discuss those stupid rules again!

And learn all about those drugs,
And why I should not hang out with thugs.

Drug tests here, and drug tests there.
Hey, this testing isn't fair!

Probation will come to check on me.
They'd know it if I try to flee.

I'll sign out, and I'll sign in.
Wow! I'm outside once again!

You know, rehab is not so bad.
In fact, I know that I'll be glad,

To one day look back and see,
Rehab was really good for me.

I've got a choice. Now I'll decide. *(choice)*
To change or not, is it my pride,

That holds me back? It seems to me,
That in rehab, I'll be free,

To come and go, get a new life,
Give up the pain, the hurt, the strife.

The drugs will go, the *frenemies* too.
I'll be different in all I do.

God will be the boss of me,
Now, and for all eternity!

I will like who I am!
And I will like it where I am!

Made in the USA
Charleston, SC
08 January 2015